CW00738844

In Search of the Moderate Muslim

Jon Gower Davies

THE
SOCIAL
AFFAIRS
UNIT

This book is dedicated to the life and memory of
Carl Pearson, a good and decent man.
We all miss him very much.

© The Social Affairs Unit 2009
All rights reserved

British Library Cataloguing in Publication Data
A catalogue record of this book is available from the British Library

All views expressed in this publication are those of the author, not those
of the Social Affairs Unit, its Trustees, Advisers or Director

The Social Affairs Unit gratefully acknowledges the support of the John
Templeton Foundation for the project of which this publication is a part

Printed and bound in the United Kingdom

ISBN 978-1-904863-37-3

Social Affairs Unit
314–322 Regent Street
London W1B 5SA
www.socialaffairsunit.org.uk

The Social Affairs Unit has no responsibility for the persistence or
accuracy of URLs for websites referred to in this publication, and does
not guarantee that any content on such websites is, or will remain,
accurate or appropriate.

CONTENTS

ACKNOWLEDGEMENTS

I am grateful to Michael Mosbacher for support in writing this book, to the Social Affairs Unit for publishing it, and to Clive Liddiard for a scrupulous editorial scrubbing and correction of my rather badly typed text. I have, over some time, imposed myself and my concerns about Islam and Muslims on Norman Dennis, Harry Averley, Ian Ness, Mavis Zutshi, Denis MacEoin, David Mayhew, John Beazley, John Taylor and Carl Pearson; and in the ensuing conversations they have been, as it were, vigorous, contentious and helpfully critical: the final product is my own.

My wife Jean – well, without her, little possible: Thank you, Jean.

INTRODUCTION

1. THE ISLAMOBORE

I am unable to report that, in writing this book, I have been able to rely upon uncritical friendly support and interest from family and friends. They were not too happy with my choice of subject matter or with my treatment of it.

That makes this Introduction rather unusual, in that it is concerned not so much with my particular views, but rather with those of a group of people who are, I venture to claim, typical of many millions of ordinary, moderate, middle-class British people like me. In this Introduction, I construct – from them, their lives and their comments – a Weberian 'ideal type' of such people: none of them share all of the characteristics I mention, but most of them share many. And I locate myself within this 'ideal type'. It is from this perspective that I write this book as – in large measure – an invitation to 'Muslims out there' to consider how their sensitivities and concerns as Muslims might 'interface' with ours.

One of the reasons why my friends were less than keen about my subject was that few of them are very interested in religion, and even fewer in so alien and opaque a religion as Islam. I had to reassure them that, when I said I was in search of the 'Moderate Muslim', this in no way meant that I was about to confront them with a theological treatise, another 'faith to faith' discussion between a putative moderate Christian and a putative moderate imam in a putative moderate mosque, a discussion or an argument about the respective merits of the Bible and the Qur'an. This book is not about Islam; it is about Muslims. *Islam is what Muslims do.* There is almost no theology in this book, no exegesis of sacred texts: the business of doing that is, as Ibn Uyayna put it, 'a source of stumbling to all save scholars' (Sunna Project website, February 2002, accessed 12 May 2008). I cannot, obviously, altogether avoid 'religion' – 'Muslim' is, after all, a religious term; but I am not preoccupied with the various branches of Islamic (or indeed Christian) theology. I use the term 'moderate' in a purely secular sense, seeking to evaluate the relationships of Muslims, theologically moderate or otherwise, to those ubiquitous middle-class citizens like my family and friends, the mainstay of our moderate body politic. I attempt as much to explain us to Muslims as Muslims to us – risking the obvious retort, perhaps, that all concerned might well regard this task as either dull, or dangerous, or beyond me.

I offer a secular, empirical discussion of Muslims, on the grounds (to repeat myself) that *Islam is what Muslims do*. Embedded dialectically in this discussion, but largely left unsaid rather than being tediously explicated throughout this book (its contrasts being rather obvious), is the world of ordinary, white, middle-class people like me.

My understanding of 'Muslims out there' is not based on extensive contact with Muslims. I have almost no Muslim friends and little personal experience of Muslims (either middle-class, like me, or working-class, of the same economic status as the people I used, as a Labour councillor, to represent). I rely, as a reason for writing this book, on that great unpleasant snowstorm of Muslim life that has engulfed us in the last 20 years or so. From that, and from a wide reading in relevant literature, asserting that *Islam is what Muslims do,* I feel able to say that Muslims and their world are thus knowable to me, my family and my friends, to whose concerns I now return, since they are a major building block of this book. I repeat, though: *Islam is what Muslims do*. There is no getting away from the radical empiricism of that. This book is about Muslims, not Islam. This is a distinction easier to make than to maintain, as, by definition, I am dealing with a section of the population of Great Britain that, in the predominantly secular world of my friends, is unusual in that it is identified by religious belief.

Over and above the ordinary groans that sought to ward off my authorial ambitions and obsessions, there was very clearly an irritation at what my friends regarded as my bringing yet further incursions of 'Muslims' into their customary lives: would I be yet another Islamobore? My friends have had enough of the Muslim presence on radio, in the newspapers, on television. Two per cent of the population was taking up far too much time, and *if they don't like it why did they come here? No one forced them...* (words expressed, if expressed at all, rather reluctantly and sorrowfully, such sentiments clashing with their deeply held liberal principles). At one level, my friends knew that what was happening to their country was wrong, very wrong; and, at another level, they were uneasy about appearing to invite charges of 'racism' or 'Islamophobia' by saying so. The bandying about of these words has had the effect of disarming my friends of their customary habit of rigorous and occasionally vigorous comment and argument: a general sense of anxiety, reinforced by an element of fear, has taken the very possibility of a rational discussion of Islam and Muslims off the middle-class agenda.

Most of my friends were (and are) opposed to the military action in Iraq, and felt that, in the context of very evident suffering in that country, it was somehow impolite to be too critical of Muslim behaviour here. There were, in addition, some expressions of concern for my safety, warnings-cum-jokes about Rushdie and *fatwas* (now, to us British, a familiar term): while usually expressed as a joke, such comments came from people who were in no way pleased that violence and threat had been injected into our daily social and political life. One way of dealing with this boredom or irritation or anger was to seek to deflect it, by taking the soft option that *'nothing objective'* could (or should?) be said about Islam or Muslims – either by me or by anyone else. This last point was legitimated by ideas derived from the world of 'multiculturalism', which, in the ranks of the Tyneside liberal bourgeoisie, now means that all cultures are sufficient unto themselves, that only their practitioners can understand, represent or 'express' them, and that (most emphatically) the once-upon-a-time hegemons among us, the agents and inheritors of the once-dominant culture, had best keep quiet and take our multicultural medicine. Furthermore, whereas by and large the beneficiaries of multiculturalism, black and minority ethnics (BMEs), have only the slogan 'institutional racism' under which to march, Islam has the additional protection of 'orientalism' – that other surrogate for *ad hominem* argument and abuse promulgated by Edward Said. We are all aware that we now live in a querulous world, in which statements and hypotheses are judged not by their own logic or reasonableness or empirical base, but by where they are coming from: *'who says?'* not *'what's that?'*

The real irritant here is not so much the ubiquity of this ideological stance, which we encounter all the time, but the fact that, at a deeper level, we – my friends and I – *know* that it is wrong and that *we* are wrong for genuflecting to it. We are all (somewhat reluctantly and inarticulately) the plodding children of Karl Popper, devotees of tentative truths painfully arrived at and discarded through ruthless, ceaseless, boring empiricism; and we know, in some dim way, that the business of maintaining such a culture, premised most adamantly on the possibility and necessity of being 'objective' (now a pejorative term), is most uncomfortable, and only too corrodible by the easier style of latter-day romanticisms, such as those offered by people like Edward Said and other postmodern solipsists. We have been forced into making confession for things we know not to be sins – and we do not like it. Most peculiarly, to our secular minds, Muslims (followers of a religion, after all) have the rhetorical habit of ascribing *all* authority to, and seeking all authority *from*, an *ad* (or *ab*) *hominem* source, the *homo* in question being their prophet Muhammad. There is no BC (BM?) in Islam. As we shall have occasion to note, this expositional device seems to be the most widespread way of settling intra-Muslim debates and discussions on every day-to-day topic, no matter how humdrum or trivial: when in doubt, ask the Qur'an and the *hadith* (the sayings) of Muhammad. There are hundreds of thousands of such *hadith*, part of the exegetical fun being disputes as to which are 'hard' and which 'soft' – indeed, which are genuine. While my friends and I live in a vaguely Christian culture, no one I know would think of so interrogating Christian religious texts for guidance on the everyday matters of everyday life.

My family and friends were among the 65 per cent of the British who, in a Pew poll (Pew, 2006a; 2006b), said that they had a generally favourable view of Muslims. Most of them had opposed the sending of troops into Iraq (though not so emphatically the sending of troops to Afghanistan). Had they known that the same poll reported that a significant majority of the Muslims living in Britain viewed us British as selfish, arrogant and violent, so guiltily liberal are they that they would probably have examined their consciences *and themselves* to find where *they*, rather than the Muslims, had gone wrong. My family and friends are mostly meritocratic, moderate, middle-class people; and, without being aware of the actual Pew poll, they are uneasy in the atmosphere created by the level of tension implicit in it.

They are worried, for example, about being accused of being 'prejudiced' – indeed, some of them found evidence of 'prejudice' in the simple fact of my 'preoccupation' with Islam. Furthermore, it is not, sadly, unusual for such folk to be irritated by Islam and Muslims because Islam and Muslims are so much in our face – sometimes terrifyingly so: why can't you and we talk about Hindus or helpful Poles (or, more importantly, about the weddings of family members or the problems of Northern Rock)? My friends would be at one and the same time a bit fed up with Muslims, and irritated and opposed to my spending yet more time on Muslims, because, I think, they felt it to be a topic of limited importance and one about whose occasionally threatening nature 'not much could be done' anyway – and probably nothing at all by me. You cannot, they felt, and perhaps *should* not say anything about other people's religion, even though, to their secular minds, 'all religions' are anyway manifestations of ancient superstitions and quarrels best forgotten. They found 'Islam' irritating because it puts back on the political agenda a topic, 'Faith', and a style of argumentation, 'Dogmatics', best forgotten.

To repeat: my family and friends are prototypically moderate members of the moderate and meritocratic bourgeoisie – lawyers, civil and public servants, small-scale property developers and business men and women, policemen, doctors, academics, clerics, local politicians, engineers, shop owners. Their families have been born and bred in this country 'from time immemorial'. They take 'being British' for granted, being relatively unquestioning of this subscription of their political loyalty to a nation state. Like me, they are aware of the dangers of 'nationalism' and are, at times, attracted to the broader loyalties of 'Europe' or 'the World'. Like me, though, they are hard put to find a securer and more reliable political entity than the nation state, embodying as it does our national culture. They are generally readers of the *Guardian* or the *Independent*, regarding my habitual recourse to the *Daily Telegraph* to be further proof of mental decline. They are predominantly a-religious (rather than irreligious or anti-religious), rather condescendingly tolerant of my own routine practice of Anglicanism, although they themselves are, of course, inevitably, and with little objection, caught up in the familiar routine patterns of the Christian year. A few of them are, indeed, vehemently 'anti-religious' – and their quarrel is with Christianity, rather than with any of the other religions the world provides: they live, after all, as most of us British people do, surrounded, annoyingly or otherwise, by the ghosts and relics and architecture of Christianity. Organised religion, whether as something they are 'for' or as something they are 'against', plays but a small part in their various identities or self-definitions. They are generally anti- (or at least not pro-) Tory, rather than dedicatedly pro-Labour. BNP attitudes are anathema to them, associated as they are with fascism and thuggery and racism. They, like me, are in effect 'lower-case liberals', taking, for example, the view that crime or deviant behaviour has 'social' causes, and that punitive attitudes to criminals or other such less fortunate, if unpleasant, individuals are inherently wrong. They regard the Empire as rather shameful, as something we are well shot of, and to whose 'victims' we owe some kind of debt. They are generally white, mono-lingual and British-born over generations without count. Their parents or grandparents will have experienced the Second World War, sometimes as soldiers (returning or otherwise), sometimes as munitions or other 'war' workers, or through the day-to-day experience of the exigencies of national danger, evacuation, rationing and scarcity. They are peacefully patriotic, if only in the minimalist sense that they will and do feel ashamed of wrongful things done in 'our' name. They take for granted the day-to-day articulations of our history, such as public statuary, street names and war memorials, inexplicitly but correctly understanding what these symbols are about, even if their precise meaning has been lost in the rummage of signs and stories that make up the history of our people and the fabric of our cities, towns and villages – of our home. They all know, simply by tracing their own descent over two or three generations, that things can be (and have been) made better by dint of individual dedication and hard work – and some luck. Journey back over, say, three or four generations, and we would find most of our ancestors labouring on the land, in kitchens, in factories or down coal mines. They know that the United Kingdom is a blessed place in which to live, and that they are well fortunate to do so. Their major foreign travel is to Europe, or to countries which themselves derive their now-dominant culture from Europe and its several centuries of overseas expansion. Many of us have relatives domiciled in, and citizens of, such countries. My family and friends are (most of the time) polite and considerate, especially to foreigners, and they are public-spirited and concerned for their children. They – WE – are the moderate citizens of a moderate Great Britain. Within their own lives, and those of their families, Muslims have, until recently, played no part at all.

Why should such moderate and polite people be so bored and irritated by my subject matter, the search for the

Moderate Muslim? Perhaps because these moderate British people are the recipients of a stream of what often seems to be self-serving and specious apologetics made for Islam by our official and semi-official leaders and opinion formers. Muslims, too, are very vocal on their own behalf. Scarcely a day goes by without some 'reminder' of the Muslim presence in our society, be this by direct experience of prolonged security measures at airports (and soon at railway stations?); or official pronouncements on the use of nice words and tortuous phrases inviting us to make complex theological distinctions between those Muslims who 'improperly invoke Islam' for their murderous activities and those who don't; or stories told in our schools about the inspirational journey of the prophet Muhammad to Medina or of the great achievements of Muslim algebraists, architects and philosophers; or of the iniquities of anti-Islamic Crusaders and their latter-day Zionist brothers; or about forced marriage and 'honour killing' (honour?!) and planning issues to do with mosques and prayerful proclamations from minarets. The sheer presence of 'Islam' on the media and in our quotidian experience cannot, though, account for the low but steady and persistent level of animosity to yet more discussion of Islam: after all, there are other frequent occupiers of air space, such as global warming or disturbing changes in our sexual and familial lives, the discussion or presentation of which do not attract such irritation and animus.

There is a serious and general unease among my friends that, in the busy activities of Muslims and in Islam (especially in an Islam like Prometheus unbound), they are forced to confront something that, as liberals, they would prefer to avoid: the possibility that there are some ideas and some behaviours that exploit but by no means express the general freedom we enjoy. Multiculturalism and post-modernity have given soft edges to all our values: so economically successful have our societies been that we have preferred to forget that our forebears had to struggle to make them so, and that, as the (true) truism has it, eternal vigilance is the price of liberty. We have become lazy in our liberalism, so unproblematic has it apparently become – a success story with no end, no need for commemorative reiteration, because such 'triumphalism' in itself refutes the nature or tone of the success. Moderate people like me and my friends would rather be busy doing things with – enjoying even – the liberties we have, rather than be compelled by a somewhat alien presence to face up to the task of reinvigorating and defending those values. We know for sure that we are moderate people. We do not know what a Moderate Muslim is. This book is an attempt at a conversation between these two co-dwelling but very different classes of people.

I will, I am reasonably confident, be able to show, empirically, that we native, moderate, British people are very different from what the Moderate Muslim is: our moderateness is not their moderateness. The greater difficulty is to work out whether these cultural differences necessarily lead from a demonstrable mutual unfamiliarity, through casual disdain and on to enmity...or from unfamiliarity, through casual curiosity and on to friendship. Here, empiricism can take us only so far, the crucial (but very opaque) matter being the relationship between small groups or gangs of violent people, the community from which they come, and the larger community of which all are part. Two of my friends, one Catholic, one Protestant, grew up in Ireland. I grew up in colonial Kenya, in a colony within a colony, confronting 'Mau Mau', but in the main having little social contact with the Africans (or indeed the Asians) who lived in the same country. We experienced violence as something that emanated both from outside our community and also (as a response) from within, aimed primarily at the violent enemies outside, but affecting everyone inside. White moderates, to whom the violence of their brethren might well be something of which they were ashamed, could do little. It was indeed dangerous to do anything – and anyway, *how* could we do anything? What could we do? And on whose behalf? The actual recipients of 'our' violence – Africans – were people with whom we had no familiarity, and of whom indeed we were afraid; whereas 'our own' violent men were, at one and the same time, at least friends of our friends (if not friends of ours), and in some dismal sense they were our protectors: we were safer, and strutted a little more securely, because of that protection. What does 'the community' – whether that of moderate Protestants or Catholics in Northern Ireland, or that of the community of moderate whites in the colonial Africa in which I grew up, or that of 1960s Mississippi where I spent some time – do about violence and the presence, among them and next door to them, of men of whose violent activities they are only too well aware? Whose side, as we used to sing, are you on?

2. WHOSE SIDE ARE YOU ON?

Just the place for a Snark! I have said it twice:
That alone should encourage the crew.
Just the place for a Snark! I have said it thrice:
What I tell you three times is true.

Lewis Carroll, 'The Hunting of the Snark'

'One of the most moderate Muslims that I have met',
said Headmistress Anne Cole of her Teaching Assistant
Zahoor Iqbal, found guilty of helping convicted terrorist
Parviz Khan in his plan to kidnap and murder a British
Muslim soldier.

Daily Telegraph, 16 February 2008

On 12 November 2007, the Daily Telegraph lead story was 'Alarm at Britain's "Broken Society"'. The story provided a panorama of school-aged children caught up in the criminal justice system, of teenagers using guns and knives, teenagers drinking and drug taking, and the general mayhem created in our society by teenagers, and by their crime and violence. The Daily Telegraph's editorial comment continued the story of family breakdown, teenage truancy, drug abuse, gang culture and alcoholism. At no point in any of this did either leader writer or reporter feel obliged or motivated to refer to the possibility or probability that most teenagers are moderate; that most people maintain moderate and steady family relationships; that most people, including teenagers, are, most of the time, moderate in their general behaviour. The rhetoric of social pathology seems able to describe the phenomena of deviancy in the British population *without* being always accompanied by defensive, proclamatory or apologetic explicit reference to the comparative moderate good sense of most of us moderate British people most of the time. The same rhetoric or literary 'trope' does not characterise our discussions about Muslims in our society. The language we use to try to comprehend Muslims presents us, simultaneously, with two kinds of Muslims. *Moderate* Muslims are, typically, called into existence to offer a redress for the public offence given by their *'immoderate'* or *'fundamentalist'* (the term varies) co-religionists, giving us *Moderate* Muslims and, as polar opposites, *Immoderate* or *Non-Moderate* or *Jihadist* Muslims or *Islamists*. The fact that Muslims are routinely presented, explicitly and tacitly, in this way underlines the fact that the presence, here in Great Britain, of Muslims and their various groups is a problem in a way in which the presence here of, say, Hindus and Sikhs, or Australians and Slovenians is not. Muslims are always in the news, and there seems to be a permanent quarrel going on. The imputed existence of (at least) two kinds of Muslims is, among other things, a rhetorical device to enable *us*, the Moderate British Majority (this term varies, too), to rest easy with the Moderate Muslims who live among us. We are, so we are invited to assume, able to rely on and find common ground *with them*, though not (in the same way, clearly) with their distinctly unpleasant co-religionists – from whom they, the Moderate Muslims, are, we are asked to believe, as estranged as we are.

What follows in a later chapter are some more, recent examples, well covered in the media, of the difficult and precarious business of making and sustaining these necessary distinctions. In these examples of reported speeches and newspaper reports we see expressed the conversations – the musings or soliloquies, even – that go on in the hearts and minds of many a moderate citizen of this country. 'Thinking about

Muslims' is concerned both with the 'objective truths' about this particular section of the population *and also* with that section's relationship with us – where 'us' is itself, of course, part of the analytical problem. When faced with the evident murderous activity of what we would like to hope is a Muslim (preferably non-British) minority, 'we' are asked to seek both consolation and hope in the putative existence of a moderate (preferably 'British') Muslim majority. This putative majority needs to have put to it the series of questions and concerns presented in this book: their moderateness cannot simply be taken as unproblematic, as something to be taken casually on trust (things have gone far too far for that). There is, for example, the problem of '*Who speaks for the moderate majority?*' when the boundaries between the moderates and immoderates seem to be constantly shifting, and when such a shift thereby reconfigures the boundaries and contact lines between 'us' and 'them'. Where, for example, on the moderate–immoderate continuum are we to place the Muslim Council of Britain (MCB)? In February 2008, the MCB issued two 'press releases', responding to the controversy occasioned by the archbishop of Canterbury's pronouncements on *shariah* law in Britain. The second press release (MCB website, 14 February 2008) referred to the MCB's expectation of 'a fair discourse free from the current shrill hysteria screaming of impending doom from invading hordes' – presumably a comment on those indigenes who read the *Daily Mail* – but then, interestingly, went on to claim that 'many of our opinion-formers have now proven to be incapable of creating a positive discourse, [so] it is down to us, at grassroots level, to dispel the misconceptions, the hatred and the divisive extremism both against as well as amongst Muslims'. This is a most interesting hint of internal Muslim 'divisive extremism', although it is glossed within the habitual proclamation of a generalised hatred which the MCB insistently presents as surrounding Muslims. Muslims are a relatively opaque community to people like the friends and relatives I have described. Muslims come from many different countries and speak several languages: 1.3 billion souls, 11,379 languages, says *Q-News*, the 'magazine for the Global Muslim' (*Muslim Directory*, 2007/08: 198). The foundational text of Islam, the Arabic Qur'an, recited or written, even when translated, is inscrutable to nearly all of us: and attempts to comprehend it are (as are similar attempts to comprehend vernacular Jewish or Christian or Hindu scripture) invariably shipwrecked on the very proper rigours of fine and contextualised translations and exegeses. Such exegeses are the domain of a very few scholars, whose very expertise then renders them incomprehensible to everyone else! At the risk of being accused of being indifferent to such scholarship, I repeat that this book is based on the simple premise that *Islam is what Muslims do* (and, to be even-handed, Christianity is what Christians do). It relies on a 'rough translation' not of Islamic texts, but of Muslim activities, as reported in casual comments, in legal cases, and in books, journals, events, newscasts, conversations. 'Rough translations' is a phrase which aptly describes the conversations that we Westerners, we Christians even, have with the alien Muslims currently living here. It may even describe the conversations we have with each other on this topic.

'Christianity', of course, has a much looser fit with 'Westerners' than does 'Islam' with 'Muslims'. Very few British people or Europeans find their primary identity in religion; and even those that do will tend to see the role of their religion in their society in a quite distinctive way. Furthermore, with Muslims (much more than with Christians or Westerners), religious scholars and their associated students and popularisers will invariably be men: 'society' in Muslim terms is generally society with and of Muslim men. An English friend of ours who had married a Yemeni Muslim (thereby becoming his second wife) brought her husband to stay with us; she then supervised my exclusion (from my own front room!) when her husband was showing family photographs. These photographs included, I was told (because I was not allowed to see), one of his first wife, unveiled: I was instructed to leave the room. As a moderate fellow, I did; but this aspect of Muslim sensitivity I do not, I have to say, regard as being moderate.

There is no need to labour this basic point: to most of us, Muslims inhabit a semi-opaque world, and one has to assume that we are rather opaque to them. Given that, one has to accept some small part of the post-modernist stance: it is currently – given a certain acerbity between natives and Muslims – almost impossible to ground a debate with a Muslim interlocutor on the basis of an anticipated routine objectivity and impartiality; and this comment, I would guess, cuts both ways. All we can hope for, right now, is some form of 'rough translation', in which we can try to find at least some plausibility (I put it no stronger than that) in the disparate perspectives and rhetoric of our respective communities. From such plausibilities we may be able to move to some objective truths about each other. Just now, though, we have, on the one hand, a semi-opaque Muslim world; and, on the other hand, there is a British, Western world, perhaps opaque to most Muslims – but relatively open and transparent to me. Between us fly loud volleys of protestations, or whispered fusillades of hopeful words and invitations. It must be possible to subject at least some of these words to various tests of plausibility. In particular, I wish to know: how plausible is the claim that most Muslims are moderate? How plausible is *our* claim to moderateness? Can I rely on these Moderate Muslims to understand the nature of my moderateness? Can I rely on them to both understand *and to defend* my moderateness and my moderate world? What range of meanings am I invoking when I insist (as I do) that 'I am moderate' and that I believe there to be Moderate Muslims – but that I do not know what, or where, or who they are, or how many there are of them? What, as moderates, do they do with or to or for their evidently immoderate violent co-religionists? What, for example, are we moderates, British or Muslim, to make of the extraordinary threat or warning uttered by Muhammad Abdul Bari, secretary-general of the Muslim Council of Britain, when he referred to what he called the 'demonisation' of Muslims by 'some police officers and sections of the media'? Mr Bari said that if this 'demonisation' continued, then 'Britain will have to deal with two million Muslim terrorists – 700,000 of them in London' (*Daily Telegraph*, 10 September 2006). Mr Bari would appear to have been responding to active police surveillance of many potentially terrorist Muslims – what does he expect? But even giving him some latitude for that, his remarks would seem to confer upon the entire Muslim population of Britain a moral plasticity, a capacity for violence that would take it well beyond the limits of moderateness. I have to assume that Mr Bari is wrong, and that he regrets what he said. I simply do not wish to take seriously Mr Bari's insistence that, unless the police and the media do what he wants, the entire population of British Muslims will spontaneously unleash war on our streets. What a dreadful thing to say! Mr Bari clearly has no understanding of moderate British people; and a major purpose of this book is to explicate, for such as Mr Bari, the internal constructions, the obdurate boundaries, of *our* moderateness.

This essay seeks to begin working out how we can come to some plausible view of the size, nature and intracommunal strength of Moderate Muslims and of their relationships with us. The 'us' in question are non-Muslim, white, British-born citizens, whose strong desire not to be terrorised or murdered is matched by an equally strong desire to be as fair and unbiased in our relationships with Muslim and other guest minorities as we are in our relationships with each other. The relative opacity of the Muslim world makes this purpose, this tension, an almost permanent part of white liberal, indeed white Christian, life. There are, of course, other people living here (other than the 'non-migrant white' people like me) who are members of different ethno-religious minorities: they may be Poles, Hindus, Sikhs, West Indians, Buddhists, Rastafarians. What they make of Muslim behaviour, or of ours, I do not know.

There are other difficulties. There are, we know, people who are white, British-born and British citizens who have become Muslim: indeed, approximately 4 per cent of Muslims living here fall into that category. There are, we assume (for there is an Ex-Muslim Council of Britain), brown or black British-born citizens, born into Muslim families, who are no longer Muslim. Too many conversations of the type we are trying to initiate get strangled at birth by oversensitivity to such niceties. This conversation is between the majority of people like us – born here, with English as the sole and natal language, white and married (perhaps even monogamously) to a white man or woman, himself or herself also British-born, and, nominally at least, Christian – and the Moderate Muslim, born in Britain or not, wherever he or she may be, and in however large or small a number.

It would be wrong for me to pretend that I come to this topic in total neutrality. How could that be? Some guide to my present views may be found in an earlier book published by the Social Affairs Unit: *Bonfires on the Ice: The multicultural harrying of Britain*. That book was part of an attempt to create some space for 'plausibility' in the 'conversations' between us, the white native-born (over many generations) British citizens, and the whole series of minority ethnic groups now resident among us. This book attempts to create some space to attend to the particular problems implicit in the presence here in Great Britain of 2 million or so Muslims. To repeat: Muslims are a problem for moderate people like me in ways that other recently arrived minorities are not. Why should this be the case? How is it possible for two communities to coexist when – to give one example – we have such wide divergences in attitudes to religion and violence? In 2006, Muslims all over the world rioted against some Danish cartoons depicting the prophet Muhammad. On 23 June 2006, the *Guardian* reported that, whereas most British people felt that the violence was due to Muslim intolerance of Western freedom of speech, only 9 per cent of Muslims agreed, with nearly 75 per cent blaming Western disrespect for Islam. From such figures, it would appear that we have imported conflict and turmoil into our country. Even on issues not (as it were) involving violence – such as sex and marriage, for example – there seem to be differences that are growing wider, thus further separating the 'moderates' in both camps.

We need to know what a Moderate Muslim is, and they need to understand the nature of our moderateness. We need to know how long a Moderate Muslim stays moderate, how actively or passively moderate they are, and (crucially) how they deal with or relate to their immoderate co-Muslims when they meet them. As a (Protestant) friend of mine said of the conflict in Northern Ireland: 'violence is as much directed inwards as outwards', and the balance between moderate Prods and violent Prods was (and is), among other things, a function of how well or otherwise inter-communal violence was seen to be working. The 'moderate middle' of Ulster Protestants (and Ulster/Irish Catholics) and Muslims alike may well be like an accordion: its size, length and volume a function of the relative strengths of the left hand of irredentist, illegitimate and immoderate violence, and of the right hand of the legitimate violence of the forces of law, order and the moderate view of things. Violence undoubtedly works; and in between the relative strengths and efficiencies of competing violences lie the constituencies of the watchful – and perhaps intimidated – moderates. We indigenous British moderates have internalised Max Weber's dictum: that the state has and should have the monopoly of the legitimate means of violence – the army abroad, the police at home. Is this as well accepted in the commonwealths of Islam? Would a Muslim moderate, knowing (or suspecting) that a co-religionist was planning some kind of outrage, report that person to the police?

Moderate Muslims need to fully understand the nature, the scope, the depth of our respect for our political inheritance, and understand what their presence here is doing to that inheritance. Some contemporary liberal writers bemoan the extent to which legislation, such as the various Terrorist Acts, diminishes the libertarian nature of that inheritance. I am just as concerned about the way in which that precious inheritance is being radically eroded by concessions to exigent and excessive Muslim 'demands'.

This irritation is not mere emotionality or (to use a favourite phrase of many Muslim apologists) 'Islamophobia'. Moderate Muslims (their angry co-religionists being clearly beyond the pale) could best begin to earn the title 'moderate'

IN SEARCH OF THE MODERATE MUSLIM

by using the term 'Islamophobia' as little as possible. They need to address the possibility that, as they engage in conversation with the many millions of moderate people, such as my family and friends, their own proclaimed moderateness may not square with the way moderateness is viewed by their interlocutors; and that, as guests in this country, they should feel obliged to examine and re-examine the basis of their proffered moderateness and to ground their conversations with their moderate hosts on the basis of understanding who we are. On a hill outside Kirkley Hall in Northumberland stands an obelisk, bearing the date 1788 and the inscription *Vindicatae Libertatis Publicae Anno Centesimo Salutis* (To the Centenary of the Achievement of Political Freedom). On the plinth of a column that dominates the centre of Newcastle upon Tyne is an inscription expressing the gratitude of the citizenry for the electoral reform of 1832, which ushered in 'a century of civil peace'. Over the years and events to which the Kirkley Hall obelisk refers – the Civil War, the Glorious Revolution, a religious settlement – and the years with which the Newcastle monument is concerned – the Industrial Revolution and parliamentary democracy – the people of Great Britain, by hard work, application, fortitude and luck, created a relatively stable, prosperous, generous and liberal society. In this long story, Muslims played little or no part. Guests, Muslim or otherwise, are welcome here – and the welcome is an offer of a gift well worth having. That is the basis of our conversation with Muslims. We will begin to be able to see them as 'moderate' when they seem able to understand that.

CHAPTER 1

THE PROBLEM STATED

We all know that the terrorists from whom we can expect further murderous onslaughts will be Muslims.

We all know that most Muslims are moderate.

CHAPTER 2

SOURCES: *SNOW* AND ROUGH TRANSLATIONS

Snow is the title of Orhan Pamuk's great disturbing novel about the journey of an Istanbul intellectual, Kerim Alakusoglu, or 'Ka', to the Turkish city of Kars. Ka had spent most of his working life in Germany. He is ostensibly in Kars to do research into the large numbers of young women who are committing suicide in protest at the secular Turkish republic's ban on the wearing of the headscarf in school. In actual fact, he is (as he frequently tells us) looking for happiness, both in general and in the shape of Ipek, a young woman he had known previously. The apparent banality of this must be seen against the background of a city in which people seem more concerned to spy on and terrorise each other than to enjoy life: there is not a lot of happiness in Kars. The city of Kars, located as it is on Turkey's eastern boundary, over by Armenia, was once Armenian, then Ottoman, then Russian, and now Turkish. Abandoned Armenian houses dot both the city and Pamuk's story; the city has an Armenian museum that simply ignores the reason why the houses are empty. In the novel, snow blankets the city, cutting it off from the rest of Turkey, and giving strange sibilant surreal emphasis to the murderous interplay of the factions and enmities of the isolated and troubled people of Kars: everything is in whispers, everything threatens. Ordinary things – like love, happiness, mutual trust and day-to-day honesty and relaxation – are trapped in the violent purposes of terrorists and of a military that is determined to trap and kill the terrorists, and, in the process, to be as violent as they are. Strange vicious 'actors' strut about the place, spinning deadly lies and dramas, and on one occasion gunning down their audience. Old liberals turn into careful cowards; children ebb and flow; women suffocate and kill themselves. The dead Armenians are, visibly, not there. Everyone seems to be a recruiting agent for some strange and ominous purpose. All the while, ubiquitous snow, with all the melting individuality of the single flake and yet the insistent and persistent sameness of the snowstorm, determines, conducts and circumscribes the behaviour of these sad and angry people in the semi-quarantined town. Ka eventually leaves the city with the promise but not the actuality of love and happiness, and is later killed for some reason connected with what he did in Kars – which was nothing of any great offence – he wanted, perilously enough, to be happy. All lives are wasted. Kars remains as it was, the events in the book merely further additions of terrorist squalor to the accumulated misery of the city.

When, in amiable, scuffling 21st-century Britain, one constructs a diary in the mind or a scrapbook presenting the details of the events of, say, the last 20 years, it can feel as if we, too, have been living in such a snowstorm. The alien city of Kars seems familiar, so grotesquely similar and so similarly unreal have been some of the events that have so unexpectedly unfolded here in our liberal, tolerant United Kingdom, where mutual trust and political safety have for so long been, so fortunately, taken for granted. I relate some of these details here, for effect as much as for information: the facts are the play, the theatre of British people, part actor, part disbelieving audience, attending to the introduction of Muslims into our society. People who find their 'facts' in novels may, in Pamuk's story about Kars, find a grim, sombre foil to considerably more jocund novels such as *Brick Lane*, or films like *Bend it Like Beckham* or *East is East*, which paint so much lighter a picture of Muslim or immigrant life in Britain. *Brick Lane*, of course, ends with the little girl inviting her mother to ice-skate (in a sari!) and dealing with the latter's objections by saying: 'This is England, you can do whatever you like.' Well, perhaps, little girl: but I gather that, when *Brick Lane* was being turned into a film, the threat of violence prevented filming on site, and Her Majesty the Queen absented herself from the premiere because of its 'sensitivity'. The Queen, of course, found herself abused when, in 2008, she knighted Salman Rushdie, who, not for the first time, found himself the object of murderous intent and threat.

The year 2006 ended (and 2007 began) with publicity about an EU report on Islamophobia: 'Islamophobia plagues Europe', said the *Muslim Weekly* (22 December 2006). The end of 2007 was marked by more alarms and excursions. The bishop of Rochester, Michael Nazir-Ali, drew attention to what he described as 'no-go' Muslim-dominated areas, into which, he said, Christians were fearful to enter. 'The nutter', said Yasmin Alibhai-Brown, a famously moderate Muslim multiculturalist; and she went on to ask how 'an immigrant priest who hails from the Indian sub-continent' could turn into a 'vicious bulldog' (*Independent*, 7 January 2008) (the bishop was born in Pakistan to Muslim parents). On the other side of the moderate divide, in Newcastle upon Tyne we saw the long-established Society for Promoting Christian Knowledge (SPCK) bookshop losing staff and facing 're-branding', having been taken over by an American Christian organisation to which Islam was the greatest threat of the 21st century. Books that are severely critical of Islam were, at the insistence of the new owners, placed on the SPCK shelves. The long-serving manager left in protest, and the SPCK is now, it seems, in the hands of receivers. In Scotland, wrote the *Muslim Weekly* on 14 December 2007, Muslims were experiencing more prejudice than they had in 2003: half of all Scots felt that Scotland would begin to lose its identity if more Muslims went to live there; and while 65 per cent of Scots were against prejudice, 29 per cent believed that prejudice could be justified 'for good reasons' (Scottish logic has long been opaque to non-Scots). But stranger things were happening in far-away Sudan.

What are we to make of the Great Teddy Bear Incident that took place near Khartoum? Did grown men really prance up and down the streets of Khartoum, waving swords and demanding the death of some well-meaning white

Englishwoman for agreeing with her pupils to name a teddy bear Muhammad? Did the president of that country, Sudan, actually say, of another Western presence in the Muslim world, that some apparently incompetent (and perhaps venal) French aid workers wanted 'to restart the slave trade by abducting Muslim children...they are a cursed alliance of Jews and Christians who bless the abuse of Prophet Mohammed as a sign of freedom of expression, all in order to fuel the conflict in Darfur' (Gerard Prunier, Open Democracy website, 5 December 2007). The president of *Sudan* is accusing Jews and Christians of wanting to get the slave trade going?! What planet are we on?

At the end of December 2007 and in spring 2008 came further news of two young men in Iran being executed for being homosexual, of a young woman being thrashed (after having been raped) for the crime of 'mingling' (i.e. being in the company of a man), and of a Newham councillor receiving death threats for voting against the proposed huge mosque at the London Olympic site. Teheran's police chief has banned high boots because they are un-Islamic. Back in Britain, the *Sunday Times* (25 May 2008) tells us that 'Islamic terrorists may be targeting mentally disturbed or disabled people to form a new "brigade" of home-grown suicide bombers'. Muslim checkout staff feel obliged (and able) to refuse to process alcohol at the checkout desk, and from Bradford Mr Besharat Rehman, owner of a *halal* supermarket, felt 'frustrated and angry' because the Walkers crisps he had been selling turned out to contain alcohol (*Times*, 22 February 2008). In the same year, Communities Secretary Hazel Blears wrote to all local authorities to urge them both to encourage Muslim women to play a larger part in society and to train them to talk their male relatives out of taking part in 'violent extremism' (*Daily Telegraph*, 24 January 2008). At about the same time, the police and others were drawing our attention to the (predominantly, but not exclusively, Muslim) phenomenon of 'honour' killings – a disgraceful misnomer if ever there was one – and Mr Rushdie, suddenly Sir Salman, found himself yet again the object of furious abuse. On this occasion, Muslim turbulence spilled over into verbal attacks on the Queen and flag-burning on the part of a small ranting mob shouting abuse at Her Majesty outside the Regent's Park Islamic Centre (which of course stands on land given to Muslims by Her Majesty's father, King George VI). On the radio one morning, I heard a most tasteless discussion between two scholarly Muslim exegetes as to whether the Muslim prophet Muhammad could or could not be regarded as condoning or encouraging the stoning of women 'taken' (as the Bible has it) 'in adultery'. Why does the BBC dignify such barbaric debates by giving them air time? Who cares what Muhammad thinks of stoning women? No one should do it, full stop. Month after month, our interactions with the Muslim world seem to throw up 'incidents' in which the apparent triviality of the offence is in reverse proportion to the vehemence and minacious dreadfulness of the response. To a moderate Western person, the very nature of such grotesque events – and, even worse, their prosaic and dispassionate 'analysis' by generally sane commentators – calls to mind those weird medieval discussions about the appropriate punishment for women who had sexual intercourse with the devil, or about the requisite tensility and lacerability of hair shirts.

Violence calls much of this language into existence. On 4 July 2006 (a year after the bombings and murders on the London Underground), a leader in *The Times* said that 'the majority of Muslims must be prepared to show leadership and not allow themselves to be intimidated by a raucous minority'. Raucous? In that same week, Prime Minister Blair, commenting on the police raid on Forest Gate, London, in which one Muslim man was accidentally shot in the shoulder, said 'I suspect that most Muslims would recognise that Forest Gate in a sense had to happen' (*Times*, 5 July 2006). Mr Blair was, of course, referring to the actual police raid, and not to the shooting; but he was doing so in the context of very noisy ('raucous') demonstrations against the police, with the new secretary-general of the Muslim Council of Britain, Dr Muhammad Abdul Bari, prominent among the objectors. As with so much comment on Muslims, we see, in both the *Times* leader of 4 July and the prime minister's words of 5 July, language used to proclaim the presence of the Moderate Muslim ('most Muslims') as a balancing – indeed dominating – counter-force to the life and style of his less accommodating 'raucous' co-religionist. Seldom can euphemism have been used so prettily as an instrument of state.

Euphemism has become government policy. Officialese and press commentary now invoke a particular image of the internal structure of Muslim society in Great Britain, as well as of its putative relationships with the population at large. Moderate Muslims must be presented as anxious to distance themselves from their 'raucous' co-religionists – in part so that moderate whites can maintain the momentum of their own moderateness and of their efforts to retain and broadcast an egalitarian and liberal attitude towards Muslims. Indeed, so desperate is this urge that violent Muslims are in danger of being denied the very *status* of Muslims, since the government and organisations such as the EU wish us to call them '*anti-*Islamic terrorists', thus detaching them completely from the religion in whose name they (speciously it would seem) kill. This (no matter what the underlying reality) is what we moderate natives would like to see: Moderate Muslims and Moderate Natives relying on each other; a united policy mission statement – as if a situation that is more an object of desire than reality is actually already in existence, so that (hopefully), through such helpful fictions, that which is desired may at some point come to be that which is. Where euphemism falters, let fancy rush in.

However hard we all try to think otherwise, violence and bombings are clearly the hard edge or underpinning of all this discussion. An Oxford University Press poll gave '9/11' as the word (*sic*) picked out by a representative sample of British people as summing up the 'mood' (the *Zeitgeist*?) of the 21st century (*Daily Telegraph*, 5 December 2007).

It is not surprising, then, that moderates such as me would have derived little solace from the findings of a Populus poll of July 2006, which stated that 'only' 13 per cent of Muslims believed the London suicide-bomb killers should be considered martyrs. Whatever the other 87 per cent felt about these killers, 13 per cent adds up to about 200,000 Muslims, resident in Britain, who apparently see religious virtue in what a gang of suicide murderers did in London. One has to assume that the 200,000 Muslims who consider the London killers to be martyrs all have family, friends and acquaintances – and that this is true also of the 2,000–4,000 or so Muslims currently under surveillance by the police. And one must assume that, in the social circles inhabited by such immoderate people, the moderate majority is busy dissuading them and, where necessary, reporting them to the police. Yet sadly, an earlier poll by the Federation of Student Islamic Societies found that one in 10 of its members would not inform the police if they learnt that their fellow Muslims were planning a terrorist attack, while a further 10 per cent declined to comment (*Times*, 22 September 2005). A later poll (*Sunday Times*, 27 July 2008) stated that just under 33 per cent of Muslim students in Britain thought that killing in the name of Islam could be justified. If to these figures we add the threat (or boast) made in 2006 (*Times*, 10 September 2006) by the MCB's Bari of being able to summon up 2 million Muslim terrorists to occupy the streets of Britain, then it is not surprising that moderate people like me see but limited potency in the Moderate Muslim.

The choice of the term 'suicide murderers' is part of my 'moderate' reaction to events in London and elsewhere. I would count myself among the 78 per cent of the general population who, according to the same poll, thought that more suicide-bomb murders were 'highly likely or likely'. Some 42 per cent of Muslims were of the same opinion. It came as no surprise to me when, in 2008, we witnessed bomb blasts in the West Country, in Exeter, the bomb being delivered by a young man from Plymouth. I assume that the 58 per cent of Muslims who did *not* expect further murderous bombing do not, therefore, feel themselves too obliged to be alert to the presence of murderers and would-be murderers in their midst. To them I must say that I am quite sure (as, clearly, are most of my fellow British citizens and a large minority of Muslims) that soon Muslims will inflict yet further murderous mayhem on our country, and that they should have known that this was likely to happen. A denial of its probability is an invitation to ignore its reality.

Hunting around for reasons for optimism, we find that, on some matters, the general population and Muslims were quite close together in the 2006 Populus poll; for example, 54 per cent of the former and 57 per cent of the latter found public drunkenness offensive (so do I), and the figures for those offended by females in low-cut tops or short skirts were 21 per cent and 29 per cent, respectively. The question of the sexual attitudes of ourselves and of the Muslims will be discussed later, in Chapter 7.

A YouGov poll in 2007 showed that 44 per cent of Londoners regarded Islam as generally tolerant, while 49 per cent believed that it was generally intolerant (*The Week*, 24 November 2007). Complaint is, of course, frequently made in journals like the *Muslim Weekly* of 'Islamophobia', which is held to underlie the opinions of people such as those represented by this 49 per cent. In such an atmosphere of mutual suspicion and social distance, we, as moderates, while capable of believing that we do have *some* things in common with our Muslim fellow citizens, are obliged (as are they) to find more.

At the same time, Moderate Muslims must, and do, make parallel attempts to separate themselves from the 'raucous' among them. On 28 November 2007, the MCB issued a press release describing as 'a disgraceful decision [that] defies common sense' the news that a Sudanese court was to try Ms Gillian Gibbons for being party to a primary-school class voting to give the name Muhammad to a teddy bear. The attempt by the MCB to 'moderate' the case was welcome, as was the 'rescue mission' of two British Muslim peers who flew out to Sudan. All this, though, was rather undermined by the decision of the Sudanese court to imprison Ms Gibbons (who could have faced 40 lashes and six months in prison) for

15 days. This verdict was too moderate for some Sudanese, and it led to demonstrations on the streets of Khartoum that both demanded and threatened Ms Gibbons' death. On top of that, the Sudanese Association of the *Ulema* (the theological experts of Sudan) proclaimed that 'what has happened was not haphazard or carried out of ignorance, but rather a calculated action and another ring in the circles plotting against Islam. It is part of the campaign of the so-called war against terrorism and the intense media campaign against Islam' (*Independent*, 29 November 2007). Whatever the views of the MCB, and whatever the publicity success of the two Muslim peers who flew off to negotiate with the Sudanese leader, the fact remains that the government of a major Muslim state condoned the imprisonment of a British guest worker for naming a teddy bear Muhammad.

The moderate views of the MCB on the issue of the Muhammad teddy bear will inevitably, in the minds of some moderate whites, be seen in the light of the not-so-moderate Sudanese *Ulema*. This clearly bothered the *Muslim Weekly*, which, on 16 November 2007, quoted with approval the comment by Jemima Khan (former wife of Pakistani cricketer Imran Khan) that 'It is important to differentiate between Islam as practised in many Muslim countries and Islam as it is in the Qur'an.' Ms Khan's well-meant (if jejune) comments raise another aspect of the moderate/immoderate problem: that of the nature (moderate? immoderate?) of the societies, states or nations from which most of our British-living Muslims are descended or actually come. In Chapter 4, I spend some time looking at some of the members of the 57 countries making up the Organisation of the Islamic Conference. How many of these countries are moderate in ways that would make us moderate British citizens feel comfortable? Put simply, how many moderate British people would like to live their whole lives in Pakistan or Bangladesh? Indeed, how many *Muslims* currently living in Britain would like to live in Pakistan or Bangladesh – or Sudan?

Another attempt by the MCB to try to define and occupy the middle ground further exemplifies the gap (and demonstrates the difficulty of closing it) between Britain's Muslim minority, 'represented' by the MCB, and the generality of the population. The *Ulema*'s grasp of world affairs quoted above – weird, surely, in moderate Western eyes? – was almost equalled by Dr Muhammad Abdul Bari (again!) of the MCB, when, in November 2007, he was interviewed by the *Daily Telegraph*. Dr Bari demonstrated that, even for Moderate Muslims (such as he officially is), it must be as difficult to understand us as it is for us to understand them. Dr Bari seems either to be ignorant of 'our island story' or determined to trash it. Dr Bari was, said the *Daily Telegraph* on 9 November, worried that Britain was becoming like Nazi Germany, when 'people's minds can be poisoned as they were in the 1930s'. It is difficult to imagine a better way of offending the moderate majority of this country. The *Sunday Express* of 11 November 2007 had as its headline: 'FURY AS MUSLIM BRANDS BRITAIN "NAZI"'. The *Express* quoted Dr Bari's deputy at the MCB, Mr Inayat Bunglawala, as saying that: 'In the 1930s all sorts of popular fictions were spread about the Jewish community. They were made into folk devils and I think the word Muslim in the UK is being made synonymous with bad news.' In an editorial, the *Sunday Express* rejected Dr Bari's views ('what utter rubbish') and went on to say:

> Dr Bari is the leader of the Muslim Council of Britain
> and claims to speak for the moderates in his community.
> But does he really? Moderate Muslims share the same
> views as the moderate majority and condemn the men of
> terror because they maim and kill the innocent.
> Extremists use religion as a cloak to hide their hatred for
> others. Nazi thugs killed all who disagreed with them –
> just like the terrorists. Moderate people of all faiths
> must stand up to their threat or thousands will die.

Dr Bari had made his remarks comparing Britain and Nazi Germany in the context of a wide-ranging interview, in which, for example, he suggested that we in Britain could and should learn from Muslim attitudes to things such as marriage, sex, alcohol, raising children, abortion, adultery, modesty in dress – all good (or not bad) points; but points that were certain to be well buried by the deep-seated resentment of a typical native British man or woman at being called a Nazi. It is surely more offensive to a moderate Briton to be recruited to Nazidom than to pretty well anything else. Dr Bari lost his standing the minute he made those remarks.

Later in the month, Paul Goodman MP joined in, being reported in the *Daily Telegraph* of 30 November 2007 as saying that 'Our moderate British mosques [are] threatened by "modernisation".' He was referring to a British government-funded scheme to reform British mosques and madrassahs through a new device called the Mosques and Imams National Advisory Board (MINAB). Through MINAB, financed by the taxpayer to the tune of several millions of pounds, the thousand or so British mosques would be invited to acquire English-speaking imams to replace the large numbers of non-English-speaking imams currently running the mosques. In this way, the imams of the mosques of England (rather than the 'al-Qaeda' imams who allegedly already speak English) would attract those young, English-speaking Muslims currently disinclined to go to the incomprehensible (because non-English-speaking) mosque. Thus, these young people would be more likely to turn towards moderateness. Mr Goodman pointed out that among the participants in MINAB was the Muslim Association of Britain (MAB), which had, he said, 'links to the Muslim Brotherhood...and Hamas'. Mr Goodman said of the MCB that its 'controversial status is well known, though it has been helpful over the teddy bear issue'. Mr Goodman felt that, contrary to the express purpose of MINAB, the inclusion in it of such organisations as the MAB and the MCB could be 'fatal to the struggle against extremism'. (It is, it has to be said, strange to see HM Government putting taxpayers' money into paying for the installation of imams, when it resolutely refuses to do very much about the cost of stipends for the clerics of HM Church.)

Whatever Mr Goodman's views on the MCB, the Islamic Council of Britain regards it as 'apostate' and 'subservient to the *kuffaar* and hence have left the fold of Islam' (Dhimmi Watch website, 7 August 2004). *Kuffaars* are us, by the way. In turn, the Sufi Muslim Council, which was formed in 2006 and claims to be mainstream, covering about 80 per cent of Britain's Muslims, is regarded by the MCB as unrepresentative and divisive. The ideological pirouetting of organisations such as the Muslim Council of Britain, the Sufi Muslim Council, the Muslim Association of Britain, the Islamic Human Rights Commission and many others is part of the larger conundrum we moderate British people face when we seek to identify, and to identify with, Moderate Muslims living, moderately, with us, in moderate Britain.

Muslims, too, confront these various problems. On 16 November 2007, the *Muslim Weekly* ('The Voice for Muslims in Britain') would seem to have solved the problem when it trumpeted: 'MUSLIMS ARE MORE TOLERANT.' By this, the newspaper editors meant that Muslims were *more tolerant than non-Muslims*. They referred to a MORI sample poll, covering 941 non-Muslims and 564 Muslims, all living in London. This poll, reported the *Muslim Weekly*, showed that 89 per cent of those Muslims surveyed believed that people had the right to live their own lives, so long as they did not prevent others from doing the same; this compared with 88 per cent of Londoners as a whole. Furthermore, said the *Muslim Weekly*, 'an overwhelming 94 per cent [of Muslims] said that everyone in Britain should have equal opportunities, compared to 92 per cent of non-Muslims'. Further analysis of the poll data by the *Muslim Weekly* compared London Muslims and non-Muslims on a variety of 'citizenship' issues – pride in the local area, law and order, religious freedom; on this, Muslims were demonstrably more positive, tolerant and open-minded – all very good news.

In the same article, the *Muslim Weekly* referred to other polls, such as a Gallup poll which showed that 'loyalty to Britain' was greater (74 per cent) among Muslims than among the general public (45 per cent); it also complained about a

YouGov poll which (to the evident indignation of the *Muslim Weekly* editors) 'suggested that at least 35 per cent of Londoners held Islam responsible for the 7/7 attacks'. The *Muslim Weekly* went on to refer to a survey commissioned by the mayor of London, which found that 91 per cent of weekly media reports portrayed Islam as 'a threat to the West'. Mr Kenneth Livingstone, then mayor of London, said that 'the vast majority of Muslims hold views in common with the rest of London about respect for the law, the value of democracy', while Respect councillor Salma Yaqoob said that 'the vast majority of Muslims want to live alongside their non-Muslim neighbours' (*ibid.*).

Such attempts at cohabitation are not, it seems to me, helped by the idiocies of such self-hating westerners as Mr Boyd Tonkin, a journalist on the *Independent*, who wrote that 'The scribblings of dreamers are catharsis, not crime' (*Independent*, 12 November 2007). Mr Tonkin was describing the trial of a Miss Samina Malik, the 22-year-old self-described 'Lyrical Terrorist', accused under the Terrorism Act of possessing records likely to be useful for terrorism. The prosecution alleged that among Miss Malik's files were firearms manuals, a *mujahideen* poison handbook and a manual for rocket-propelled weapons. She was a poet, having allegedly written the following ode to throat-cutting and beheading:

> It's not as messy or as hard as some may think
> It's all about the flow of the wrist.
> Sharpen the knife to its maximum.
> And before you begin to cut the flesh
> Tilt the fool's head to its left.
> Saw the knife back and forth.
> No doubt the punk will twitch and scream.
> But ignore the donkey's ass.
> And continue to slice back and forth.
> You'll feel the knife hit the wind and food pipe.
> But Don't Stop.
> Continue with all your might.

About now you should feel the knife vibrate.
You can feel the warm heat being given off.
But this is due to the friction being caused...

The case against Miss Malik was dismissed on appeal, but not before some extraordinary effusions from her defenders. Mr John Burton, Miss Malik's lawyer, felt that her poetry was in the tradition of Wilfred Owen (*Times*, 9 November 2007). Mr Tonkin, in the *Independent*, demonstrating a somewhat broader frame of literary reference, felt that if Miss Malik was culpable, then so was President Sarkozy of France for singing the sanguinary *Marseillaise*, or so indeed was anyone who sang the *Red Flag* or read or possessed a copy of the *Iliad* or the *Song of Roland*. Miss Malik's alleged thoughts on beheading ('it's not as messy or as hard as some may think, it's all about the flow of the wrist') were, said Mr Tonkin, 'rather like a sexual fantasy gone astray'. Mr Tonkin's dangerous nonsense is about as enlightening as the Sudanese persecution of a decent well-meaning English woman and her teddy bear.

Mr Tonkin is demanding greater tolerance than liberal, moderate people like me can allow him. Mr Tonkin expresses *in extremis*, as it were, a liberal position that leaves us struggling to comprehend, let alone cope with, an inclination to commit violence that cannot be regarded as either remote from Islam or as something that demonstrates merely a general human predisposition to violence. I possess copies of both the *Iliad* and the *Song of Roland*: I have sung both the *Marseillaise* and the *Red Flag*. I can conceive of no circumstance in which, whether as a teenager with sexual fantasies or as someone fully immersed in the cultural values and classical tradition of the West, I would rejoice, even in theatrical play, in the idea of cutting someone's throat on television or in urging the bombing of trains and the killing of civilian passengers on the London Underground or at Glasgow airport. Mr Tonkin may be just a young and rather inexperienced young man, set fair, it would seem, to make a fool of himself; but he writes for a major British newspaper, part of the West-hating media that corrode our basic values.

Miss Malik, alleged devotee of throat-cutting, initially received a short suspended sentence, which was overturned on appeal. Less fortunate, perhaps, was the fate of the 'Secret Santa', Pc Rob Murrie of the Bedfordshire Police. Pc Murrie, at a staff police party, gave a Muslim colleague a Christmas present as a joke – a packet of bacon and a bottle of wine. The recipient, Pc Arshad Mahmood, though somewhat bemused ('funny', but 'a bit below the belt'), made no formal complaint. But someone did, and Pc Murrie felt obliged to resign, saying that, while he thought political correctness had gone too far, 'the force has to make decisions acting within that climate'. Senior police at the force agreed, saying that Pc Murrie's decision to resign was 'welcomed by the force'. Pc Mahmood said that he still regarded Pc Murrie as 'a good officer and a good friend' (*Daily Telegraph*, 15 January 2008). Pc Mahmood is clearly a Moderate Muslim: he should have done more for his friend; he should have been careful of his welfare and happiness. Who benefits from such a farce?

Pc Murrie will probably never again trust either his own sense of humour or Pc Mahmood. In *Snow*, Pamuk describes a city, a culture, in which fear and falsity have destroyed all possibility of trust between its citizens. The people of Kars lie about their pasts, they lie to each other, they know neither what they want nor what they once had – and ubiquitous terror, promoted by small immoderate groups, makes ignorance and denial by far the safest public stance to adopt. Towards the end of *Snow*, Pamuk gives us the following exchange between Ka, the embodiment of self-deceiving moderateness, and Blue, the Islamist terrorist who is awaiting execution at the hands of the Turkish military. Blue says:

'It doesn't matter where you live – here, or in your beloved Europe – you'll always be imitating them; you'll always be grovelling.'

'If I'm happy, that's all I care about.'

'You can go now,' shouted Blue. 'And know this: people who seek only happiness never find it.'

CHAPTER 3

PHILOSOPHIES OF HISTORY

> Islam's impact on the Christian world cannot be
> exaggerated. Islam's conquests turned Europe into
> Christianity's main base. At the same time the great
> swathe of Muslim territory cut the Christians off from
> virtually all direct contact with other religions and
> civilizations... Europe is inconceivable without
> Muhammad.
>
> Davies, 1996: 257–58

Human beings seem determined to produce dramatised pedigrees, in which facts are cloaked in both retrospective and
prospective ambition, so as to confer moral purpose on what
would otherwise be mere existence. These are the stories told
around the proverbial ancestral campfire: part truth, part
brag, part baloney. The epic poetry of ancient Babylon or
Greece, the 'histories' of Herodotus or Thucydides, mytholo-
gies such as those of the Hindus, the Celts and the Norse people, the accounts of the first Muslims – all seek to understand
and embroider the great sweeps of time, the actions of God or
of the gods, and of human involvement in it all – 'the envious
chain of destiny', as Lucan put it centuries ago. The stories are
more legend than fact, more promotion than description.

Islam has been prolific in the production of such philosophies of history – indeed, its foundational document, the
Qur'an, is such a thing – a book proclaiming the universal
truths of one religion, but very evidently redacted through the
experience of the proto-Muslims and their leaders, told and
retold in the *Sunna* and the *hadith*. From inception, the

Qur'an expresses, in its injunctions and its attendant legends, one of the major features of Islam – that it is always 'somewhere else': from the beginning it was, and is, a religion and story of 'travel', of migration and re-migration, of *hijrah* and *haj*. Inevitably, therefore, it has been an argumentative culture, always in contention with other cultures and with rival philosophies of history – more of this later. Given the conflicted nature of its origins, much of the moralising of its history has to do with the nature and prosecution of conflict, of war and military matters, of territorial aggrandisement, of imperial victories and imperial defeats – in particular, of struggle with the West.

'The West' or 'Europe', too, has its histories, its own collective hagiography – including a mythology of its very origins. Since it is with 'Europe' or 'the West' that Islam has contended and now contends, some sense of what the West and Europe represent will also illuminate what it is that Islam resents, despises and dislikes; what it saw and what it sees as the rival actor on the world stage. Interestingly, 'the West' does not see its history as so constructed; it sees its history primarily as a struggle with a less propitious past:

> Nobody who has paid any attention to the peculiar
> features of our present era will doubt for a moment that
> we are living at a period of most wonderful transition,
> which tends rapidly to accomplish that great end to
> which indeed all history points – the realisation of the
> unity of mankind... Gentlemen, the Exhibition of 1851
> is to give us a true test and living picture of the point of
> development at which the whole of mankind has arrived
> in this great task, and a new starting point from which
> all nations will be able to direct their further exertions.
> Prince Albert, in Bury, 1955: 330

This speech by Prince Albert, in the year leading up to the Great Exhibition, expresses as well as any single quotation the extraordinary confidence – extraordinary cheek, if you like – of a 19th-century European, as he stood on the threshold of an age in which European technology and imperial power would drive the world into at least some kind of unity, creating – eventually and by serendipity as much as by design – the basis for that geographical division of the world into the 200 or so post-imperial nation states that now make up the politics of the planet. Albert was unhindered by modesty or multiculturalism: to us it would be amazing indeed for one white man to claim, in an after-dinner chat at the Mansion House, to be able to speak on behalf of all human beings, and to assure them that they were all set to progress down the same track pioneered for them by enlightened Europeans.

Not 10 years before (and in their own distinctive way), Marx and Engels also saw the history of the world in the history of the West – the end of, not least, the 'idiocy of rural life', then the condition of the bulk of humankind:

The bourgeoisie has subjected the country to the rule of the towns. It has created enormous cities, has greatly increased the urban population as compared with the rural, and has thus rescued a considerable part of the population from the idiocy of rural life. Just as it has made the country dependent on the towns, so it has made barbarian and semi barbarian countries dependent on the civilised ones, nations of peasants on nations of bourgeois, the East on the West.

The bourgeoisie, during its rule of scarce one hundred years, has created more massive and more colossal forces than have all preceding generations together. Subjection of Nature's forces to man, machinery, application of chemistry to industry and agriculture, steam-navigation, railways, electric telegraphs, clearing of whole continents for cultivation, canalisation of rivers, whole populations conjured out of the ground – what earlier century had even a presentiment that such productive forces slumbered in the lap of social labour?

Communist Manifesto, website

The secular idea of human progress underpinned these ideas and philosophies. The West, even in its religion, is secular. The idea of Progress and of Enlightenment dominated Western secular thought and Western optimism for the best part of two centuries. Along with rural life and oppression would go the religions and fantasies associated with them: progress was inevitable; technology and technique would abolish superstition. Now, of course, nearly 200 years (and several savage terrors) later, Westerners, and Europeans in particular, lack that confidence, that self-admiring optimism, now seen as insolent, parochial, wrath-provoking, dangerous, foolish pride. Our recent history (of, say, the last four generations), while one in which material wealth has flowed so apparently easily, has seen the destruction of European triumphalism and a radical recasting (if not total removal) of the idea of unilinear, European-led human progress towards peace and unity. What J. P. Stern says of Central Europe can be said of all of it: 'There are no Central European patriots... There is much that is tragic and much that is absurd about the recent history of this ill-defined territory, and often it is difficult to tell which is which' (Stern, 1992: 1). So long now has it been since our captains and our kings departed, so long since we apparently sank well below the level of Nineveh and Tyre, so long since we became a little, squabbling and greedy people, that we lack sufficient belief in our competence and values to persuade ourselves (let alone others) that we are worth very much. We have settled for a comfortable, grubby, anxious fatalism:

> What is most peculiar about our age is the conviction that evil is installed at the core of history and our frenetic rejection of that conviction... The history of the last century, that *hortus inclusus* of which we remain unconscious prisoners, is so full of misfortunes on which to meditate that we sometimes feel the weight of the dead mowed down by wars and revolutions, wandering like ghosts through our cities demanding justice. As for the future, it seems opaque or even

obscure: all projects appear vulnerable, as peace appears precarious.

Delpech, 2007: 175–76

It does not do, of course, to regard as definitive the somewhat abstruse comments of intellectuals; but in the observable, day-to-day life of the Europeans (and, in a different way, of the Americans) we see a hedonistic culture that is indifferent and hostile to its own past, preoccupied with the present, and distinctly unoptimistic about the future – a passive and tip-toeing culture, devoid of the confidence of Prince Albert and Karl Marx, smug in its enjoyment of wealth and security it has not earned, a consumer society with little ambition for itself. A survey of 1990 showed that only 43 per cent of Europeans said they were willing to fight for their country, while 52 per cent of Europeans had either little or no confidence in their armed forces – the figure for 'no confidence' ranging from 19 per cent for the UK to 68 per cent (!) for the Netherlands (Davies, 1995: 85). Given the craven and dishonourable behaviour of the Dutch troops at Srebrenica, the Dutch public's views are well founded. While martial proclivities are only one mark of the vigour of a community, it is a significant one, especially when related to other aspects of European life, such as low and declining marriage and birth rates, sexual promiscuity, high crime rates, general deferment of first births (and many of those out of wedlock), high and routine consumption of drugs and alcohol – this is a picture of a culture of great wealth, perhaps, but of small, sleek and fractured horizons.

The Enlightenment has not, of course, simply gone away, leaving no trace. Paradoxically, as I argue in Chapter 6, the ideas emanating from people like Condorcet, Diderot, John Locke, David Hume and others have taken root in the religions and Churches they so pungently and effectively attacked. In essence, a Western Christian now sees, as part of his own story or interpretation of history, the propriety of the privatisation of his own faith and religious practice: there are no theocrats in Europe. This may well have 'weakened' faith

– and in a way it is this weakened semi-secularised faith that seems to give Moderate Muslims most difficulty.

It is with this semi-secular, softly religious, pessimistic yet successful Western culture that Islam has been and is in contention. It is a culture in which increasing numbers of Muslims live – or, more accurately, *choose* to live. Muslims do not share in cosmic *angst*. Not only is it someone else's *angst*, provoked by someone else. More triumphantly, from someone else's despair rises the promise of Islam. 'In the East as in the West', writes Tariq Ramadan,

> our epoch gives rise to the greatest famine ever noticed on earth. Tortured bodies echo the suffering of minds. Bodies and hearts are thirsty for humanity. Poverty, straying, dictatorships and wars stifle and stammer the dignity of several billions of men and women every day. Solitude, individualism, moral misery, and lack of love eats into the being of all those whom comfort should have made content... How, at the heart of this agony, do we respond to our hearts and protect the spirituality that makes us be? How, on the precipice of so much imbalance, do we bring forth the balance and harmony that will appease our hearts? How do we remain faithful to the pact of origin when modernity renders us so unfaithful to our humanity?... [While] the tearing apart of the Muslim world is there... The world of Islam is vibrating at this end of the twentieth century as it was vibrating at the beginning of the seventh; God is witness of the strength of faith. The mosques open up, the roads are mosques, and the earth is a mosque. The Umma is here; the rich and the poor, the computer scientist and the unlettered, witnesses of the same testimony, looking to quench the same thirst.
>
> Ramadan, 2004: xv–xvi

Ramadan is quite a favourite in liberal Europe. He is no blunt Islamic imperialist, but is an Oxford academic, a man quoted approvingly by (among others) the archbishop of

Canterbury in his famous 'Shariah' speech of February 2008. Ramadan is a man well embedded in Islam through his father and grandfather, founders of the Muslim Brotherhood, and he presents himself as engaged in the task of 'reconciling' Islam and the West – see Caroline Fourest's account of his role (Fourest, 2008).

Less well known (to most Europeans anyway) are Dr Ali Shari'ati and Dr Abdullah Hakim Quick. Dr Shari'ati, who died in 1977, was the intellectual descendant of a series of Muslim intellectuals, and a major influence in his birthplace of Iran. Here is a snapshot of his philosophy of history.

In 1972, Dr Ali Shari'ati gave a lecture in Iran on Qur'an Surah 30, 'al-Rum', 'the Romans/Byzantines and the Persians'. I offer a section of this lecture. Shari'ati describes the victory of a rag-tag band of desert warriors over the then superpowers of Rome/Byzantium, and he invokes that example as an equivalence for present-day Muslims surrounded by the seductions and perils of the West:

Throughout the world, plots have been devised to preoccupy and destroy the young generation – 'the freedom of sex'... I hope soon to see the day when the present state of affairs, which is coloured by pessimism, cursing and evil teaching perpetuated among Muslims by the enemies of Islam in order to instigate trouble between them so that they can forget the real enemy, will be transformed... I will attempt to delineate a common goal and strategy which should be adopted by Muslims throughout the world. [Tell how] a small and impoverished group of people were victorious over strong powers... They found faith and hope in themselves and realized that the East is a wild wolf while the West is a rabid dog. They realized that because the East and the West were overwhelmed by the desire for additional colonies, aggression, selfishness, fascist behaviour and exploitation, they inevitably gave birth to corruption, nihilism, aimlessness, worthlessness. Eventually, those 'great' superpowers were overthrown by a group of poor and oppressed people who came from a deserted area of the earth... The present generation of Muslims can rule the world if they know Allah, understand the world and discover the great values that Allah has bestowed upon them. With a strong spirit they can overcome the powers and become the world's leaders during this generation... The believers must be patient and show resistance. The promise of Allah is true. The believers should not allow non-believers to change their minds or alter their positions.

Shari'ati, 1986: 71–101

There are some familiar themes here: the false 'freedoms' and corrupting sex-obsession of the West; the use of the West as comparator; the claim of the deliberate subversion of Muslims by 'the enemies of Islam'; the threat-cum-warning of the coming triumph of a resurgent Islam, retrieving its once all-conquering dominance among the nations of the world. Consistently, Islam is contrasted with the West – the corrupt, on-its-last-legs West, as compared with the community of the simple but superior martial virtues of the original Muslim desert warriors. This version of military prowess is, of course, of particular relevance today, when it is not the massed armies of competent Muslim states that can threaten violence on the West, but the smaller bands of self-chosen, self-sacrificing martyrs or *jihadis*. No Muslim state, or even confederation of states, can at this time match the conventional military power of the West. Small or smallish bands of Muslim warriors – terrorists to us, brave heroes to many Muslims – have a long-standing reputation in Muslim mythology. Part of the drama of this contention with the West lies in this repeated invocation of the small group of fierce Muslim desert warriors who overcome superior forces through their own simple virtues. The great Arab historian Ibn Khaldun (who grew up in Muslim Spain), writing in the 14th century, described 'desert life [as]...the reason for bravery... Superiority comes to nations through enterprise and courage. The more firmly rooted in desert habits and the wilder a group is, the closer does it come to achieving superiority over others' (Ibn Khaldun, 1958: 282–83). Professor Mahmoud Sieny tells us that Salahuddin, the 'charitable liberator of Jerusalem', was inspired by these stories of 'the early Muslims who had gone out of the desert and defeated the two greatest empires on earth' (Sieny, 2000: 279). This image of the superiority of Muslim arms, as based on small but righteous military units, reappears again in present-day re-visitings of accounts of the Muslim 'arrival' in Andalus or Spain. I should stress that the 'truth' or otherwise of these stories is not the issue; their power lies in their telling and re-telling.

A 1996 publication repeats the claim that the Muslim forces led by Tariq ibn Ziyad consisted of between 12,000 and 17,000 men, while those of the Catholic monarch Roderick were 100,000 strong (Thomson and Ata'ur-Rahim, 1996: 14). King Roderick is further identified as being a rapist and a tyrant over his own people, while Tariq is soon welcomed by the liberated indigenous Andalusians.

The 'liberation' described in the 1996 volume by Thomson and Ata'ur-Rahim consisted of saving the 'Unitarian' Christians both from a corrupt king and from the predatory activities of their 'Trinitarian' co-religionists. After having carried out their task of liberation, the Muslims settled down to 'a simple and uncomplicated life of industry and worship which drew its inspiration from the example of the first community which had gathered around the Prophet Muhammad in Madina' (*ibid.*: 34). The 1996 account, issued by an American-based Muslim publishing house, quotes very extensively from the Spanish scholar de Gayangos (1809–97). The quotations are, in fact, part of de Gayangos' *translation* of al-Makkari's *Muhammadan Dynasties in Spain*. The Muslim imam and writer al-Makkari lived between 1591 and 1632, and his *Breath of Perfume from the Branch of Green Andalusia* and other works were written quite specifically to glorify the Muslim presence in Spain. He is one of many early writers summoned up from the past to highlight the role of Andalusia in the reconstruction and re-representation of the high purpose of Islam in world history, there being little apparent reservation about the accuracy (or otherwise) or the partisanship of these texts. The 1996 authors were concerned to emphasise

> the parallels that exist between what happened to the Muslims in Spain during the last two centuries of their rule there – the fifteenth and sixteenth centuries AD – and what has been happening to the Muslims throughout the world in the last two centuries – the nineteenth and twentieth centuries. The similarities and the underlying causes were only too obvious.
>
> *ibid.*: vii

Islam is an empire. Unlike the West, it cannot and does not surrender empire, move on, abandon empire and flourish, because empire is what Islam is. Any part of the world that was once Muslim is seen as forever thus – a credo which, among other things, creates innumerable flash-points between Islam and the West, because it is the West that has pushed Islam out of the lands it once occupied.

To return to Ibn Khaldun and the brave and virtuous desert warriors. He may well have been right about their military prowess; but he also went on to comment, in terms generally ignored by present-day Muslim celebrants of the great historian, that 'the places that succumb to Arab rule are quickly ruined' (Ibn Khaldun, 1958: 302). The 11th-century Muslim historian of early Mughul India, Alberuni, had also commented on the 'utter ruination [of] the prosperity of the country' consequent upon the Muslim invasion of India (Alberuni, 2003: 5). Alberuni was a court historian, generally (and most sensibly) very careful indeed in his criticisms of his patrons, Mahmud of Ghazni and his successor, Masud, the Mughal conquerors of India. Of their military exploits, he says that, in the face of the Muslim attack, the indigenous Hindus 'became like atoms of dust scattered in all directions... Their scattered remains cherish, of course, the most inveterate aversion towards all Muslims' (*ibid.*). Hundreds of years later, with this 'aversion' still in evidence, Sir Syed Ahmed Khan, in 1881, felt obliged to warn the majority Hindus not to expect to inherit India if and when the British left, as his 'Muslim brothers, the Pathans, would come out as a swarm of locusts from their mountain valleys and make rivers of blood flow from their mountains to Bengal' (Sharma, 1998: 19–22). It is perhaps slightly unfair to attach to these various comments Osama bin Laden's 'sermon' *Among a Band of Knights*, in which he, too, glorifies the exploits of a band of 'young believers with dishevelled hair and dusty feet', who on 9/11 'rubbed America's nose in the dirt and wiped its arrogance in the mud' (bin Laden, 2005: 194). There are, of course, liberal Muslim commentators who (genuinely, I think) seek to effect a resolution of what is, surely, a culture clash between the martial propensities of Muslims and the semi-pacific civil culture of present-day Europeans; yet even these liberal Muslims seem unable to resist the allure of the 'desert warrior' myth. In a book with which I shall end this chapter, Tim Winter (aka Abdal Hakim Murad) deplores 'piacular rites of protest' of 'the [Muslim] radicals in our inner cities' (Seddon *et al.*, 2003: 20–21). Dr Winter sees such extremism as un-Islamic and as something which, he says, will 'disappear because no-one who has a future really desires it'. Yet he concludes this analysis with what seems to me to be an extraordinary and most weird metaphor, conferring a heroic status and historical – indeed, super desert-warrior – prominence on such extremists, which they most definitely do not deserve. He says: 'the current wave of zealotry will, I have no doubt, pass away as rapidly as it came, perhaps after some climacteric Masada' (*ibid.*). Masada, of course, was the desert fortress besieged by Rome in 74 AD, after the destruction of the Temple. Masada was the scene of the collective suicide (*not*, note, suicide bombing or killing, which is murder by any other name) of the 1,000 or so Jewish men, women and children who, faced with the might of the Roman army, chose to kill themselves rather than submit to Rome. I am at a loss to see either how this invocation is justified or why it should be presented to us (as it undoubtedly is) as a form of reassurance to us here in Britain! Is the Roman army laying siege to Bradford? Winter's metaphor, unwittingly or otherwise, confers a totally undeserved heroic status upon those violent co-religionists of his, with whom he clearly disagrees. Yet his metaphor makes some forlorn sense only if we see in it evidence for the continuing potency of the Muslim mythology of the heroic desert warriors of early Islam. Beyond that, there is nothing at all to link the Jews at Masada to the murderers who killed civilians by bombing buses in London.

The 'small desert band' myth, which perhaps started with the military exploits of Muhammad in his peregrinations between Mecca and Medina, has the further effect of locating simple Muslim virtues in the form of an Arab male. Nearly all the *Heroes of Islam*, a publication of the Darussalam Publishing House, Riyadh, are Arabs and male (Sieny, 2000). Further, the imagery of the small band of simple desert warriors is in some way compatible with the oft-repeated phrase 'Islam is peace'. When small bands of simple desert horsemen emerge to triumph over and reform (by liberating, if necessary) large and opulent empires, then they can always be seen as never aggressive, always valiant, always giving generous peace terms to their 'liberated' foes, who then turn to Islam. There is, in Damascus, a huge statue of a mounted Salahuddin (Saladin), his horse rearing over the cowering and humiliated figures of Crusader knights, huddled over the sacks of loot they came to steal. The imagery is obvious: despicable thieving Westerners; heroic honest Muslim warrior. *Heroes of Islam* has a chapter on Saladin ('Salahuddin al-Ayyubi'), entitled 'The Charitable Liberator of Jerusalem'.

In my last chapter I explore yet another mobilisation of this 'desert warrior' trope, but now I turn to the contemporary historian, Dr Abdullah Hakim Quick, who prefers to set to one side the stories, legendary or otherwise, of the military exploits of the early 'desert' Muslims. Dr Quick's general theme is to consider the history of the world as, in essence, consisting of the primeval archaeology of Islam, the hidden story of Muslim 'messengers' obeying the Qur'anic injunction to spread Allah's teaching over the whole world.

This civilisatory mission is a story that came to be deeply and deliberately buried by the duplicities of 'Orientalist' Westerners, but it is there to be uncovered and re-glorified by assiduous Muslim scholars – like himself. I quote first from a transcript I made from a DVD that records a lecture given to the Daawah Association of Western Australia, and then from another given to a similar organisation in Florida (available as the DVDs *Islam, Past, Present and Future* and *The Devil's Deception in the New World Order*). Dr Quick insisted

that Muslims, obeying the injunction to spread their faith by the conversion of others, had ensured that every nation, every land received a Muslim messenger – Australia, America, Europe, Asia. Muslims were present in the Americas well before Columbus, the oldest map of America (950) is Arabic. There are Arabic words embedded in the 3000 BC royal tombs at Egyptian Saqqara, and Muslims travelled the entire earth and synthesised the cultures of Ancient Egypt, China, India, the Romans, the Greeks and the Middle East. Cordoba of Muslim Spain was the greatest city of the world – when London and Paris were villages. Islam is growing by leaps and bounds – the second largest religion in the USA, where 300 000 prisoners embraced Islam; and in the USA Muslims have lots of babies, and by holding on to their Islam Muslims will become a signal force in America. Here, in America, if Muslims unite, by the use of *hikmah* (intelligence) we can help Islam all over the world, as America is affecting all the Muslim countries, and America, through us, could come to love Islam. Islam is growing in Japan (the second largest religion), the UK, Norway, Sweden, Germany.

'Can you imagine', he said, 'Japanese Muslims!':

Take Japan and we take the world! The Japanese will get us together the kamikaze spirit into jihad! Look out world!! Islam is successful because it does not connect to one nation or race or linguistic group or caste. Allah made humanity naturally one. All creation is one, and is Muslim – the Sun, the Moon, the Planets are all Muslim.

Dr Abdullah Hakim Quick is a theologian as well as a historian. The Qur'an, in Surah 2, 115 and 213, clearly requires the practice of *da'wah*, the carrying out of an ancient and conversionary global mission by Muslims. When such peregrinations are presented as 'fact', as they are by Dr Quick, then this clearly lays the demographic foundation for the global *imperium* of Islam. By the time the West embarked on its global travels, and wherever they got to, Muslims were there already. Dr Quick's message is very clear: all that was good in the past was Muslim, actually or immanently, and all that will be of the future will be Muslim too – if Muslims can discover and recover their essential global unity and avoid internecine quarrels. There is no 'BC' in Islam (no 'BM' rather). History, past, present and future, is subsumed into the prophet Muhammad; all things begin and end with him. Everything, whether it happened before his advent or since, is related to Muhammad: everything before is annexed; everything after is attached to him, his life, his teachings. Dr Quick's 'history' is another prospective-active pedigree, a pedigree-in-the-making, as it were, re-recruiting the once glorious, if hidden, past to the equally glorious future, a future of global Islam. History writing is not mere nostalgia: what was, which was Islam, will be again.

Dr Quick is not alone in seeing things like this. 'The message of Islam', wrote Kalim Siddiqui, another prominent Muslim and the director of the Muslim Institute in London,

> is timeless and universal. So long as there exist 'political' or any other form of human organizations that do not recognize the supremacy of Allah and are unjust and oppressive, it is the duty of the Islamic movement to bring them to justice and to end oppression... The size of the Islamic movement is the entire *Ummah* knit together by the network of mosques and other

organizations throghout the world... The basic unit of Islam is the individual and there are a thousand million of them.

Siddiqui, 1983: 8, 26

Siddiqui's essay was entitled 'Struggle for the Supremacy of Islam'. There is no diffidence in these proclamations about Islam's presence in, and righteous domination of, the world. Mission and conversion (*da'wah*), conquest too, are duties of the Muslim. Often, this process is seen as one of recovering for Islam something that had been lost due to the cupidity or (temporary) success of enemies and/or faction among Muslims. A typical example concerns 'Andalus' (Spain), where the focus ignores its pre-Islamic, non-Muslim status, and instead presents it as quintessentially Muslim. Osama bin Laden, for example, describes 'al Andalus' as 'stolen Islamic land...lost because of the betrayal of rulers and the feebleness of Muslims' (bin Laden, 2005: 14). And the two Muslim authors of the book *Islam in Andalus* (quoted above) conclude a long account of what they consider to be the disaster of 'post-Muslim' Spain:

Today there are again Muslims in Andalus and their numbers are growing. One of the meanings of Andalus in Arabic is 'to become green at the end of summer' – and *insh'Allah* the long dry summer of the last five centuries in Europe is drawing to its close. Life goes on – and nothing can stop it! There is no God. Only Allah. Muhammad is the Messenger of Allah.

Thomson and Ata'ur-Rahim, 1996: 262

The idea of the political nation state – the political entity that has, for 300 years, monopolised the loyalties of Europeans – does not have any similar function in Islam. Kalim Siddiqui is quite clear: 'The nation-States where Muslims live today are the aquarium-like enclosures where the Muslims are in fact denied their freedom' (Siddiqui, 1983: 9). The primal band of desert warriors, led by the Muslim

prophet Muhammad, transformed itself into a series of imperial dynasties, more Sultanates than Caliphate, underpinned
by, and promoting the spread of, the *Ummah*, the world-wide
spread of Muslims. (Neither the Caliphate nor the *Ummah*
could prevent the most savage of fratricidal wars and killings
between Muslims – wars and killings that continue; and, of
course, the Caliphate was eventually abolished by a Muslim.)
The 'nation states' of the Muslim world, like Saudi Arabia or
Jordan, are still today dynasties rather than nations; and even
within states such as Pakistan and Bangladesh political loyalties flow to and from the mini-dynasties of tribal leaders.

The Muslim empires are, as we have seen, golden hege-
monic ages of culture and conquest, to whose return the
Muslim looks forward. There is no sharing in the guilt we liberal Westerners feel about the imperial venture; no sense that,
like us, Muslims should be perhaps wryly and cheerfully self-
congratulatory at having got out of such things relatively
easily. Where Western nations seem to want to 'move on'
from their imperial pasts, Muslims seem to wish to recover
and relive them – and there is anger in the nostalgia.

Islam is both *hijrah* and *haj* – a going out and a coming
in, a settling in and a moving towards; and in its sense of history, this fluidity – be it of the first simple 'desert' Arabs and
their successors, or of major 'migrations' to Asia and India,
then to Europe and America – gives it a ready-made set of
rules, a blueprint for settlement and, hopefully, eventual domination. This needs to be stressed: migration and settlement is
what Muslims have always done and continue to do, and do
very competently. They are suppliants nowhere, but seasoned
settlers everywhere; and the source of this present-day competence is in the endlessly repeated accounts of their earlier
doings, which legitimate their movement over the face of the
earth.

I conclude this chapter on 'Philosophies of History' with
an account of one attempt, made by Imtiaz Ahmed Hussain,
a Muslim academic, to apply the old stories of Muslim *hijrah*
to the new story of the *hijrah* to Great Britain, one of the
many new lands to which Muslims have recently migrated.

The story is told in 'Migration and Settlement: A Historical Perspective of Loyalty and Belonging', being pages 23–37 of Mohammad Siddique Seddon's book *British Muslims: Loyalty and Belonging*, a book containing essays and conference papers by, as far as I can see, Moderate Muslims. I return to this book and this particular story in the concluding pages of this book. I have to say that both there and here I stand amazed at the sheer idiosyncrasy of the argument – and it is an argument, not just a history. The simple importation of so distant a past is itself part of the argument: at the time of the *hijrah* to Abyssinia in 615 CE, King Ethelbert ruled Kent – is that relevant to any contemporary issue?

The story, as told in 2002/03, relates how, in 615 CE, a hundred-strong band of persecuted and frightened asylum-seeking Muslims was given permission by Muhammad to go to the Christian empire of Abyssinia for safety. At the time, Muhammad's domestic success and personal safety were in doubt: his followers were being persecuted and killed. Later, when Muslim dominance was established in Arabia, the 100 or so Muslims went home – although Ahmed Hussain does not, interestingly enough, mention this. He tells us that 'Abyssinia' (modern-day Nubia, Ethiopia, Eritrea, Sudan and parts of Somalia) was a place well known to Arab traders and 'indeed, some of the earlier Prophets had made the *hijrah* to Africa, not least Abraham, Joseph and Jesus' (*ibid.*: 24). (Abraham, according to the Qur'an 3:67, was a Muslim.) Abyssinia, a predominantly Christian country ruled over by the Emperor Negus, is described by Hussain as 'the most politically sophisticated unitary kingdom in Africa'.

In Negus' Abyssinia, the migrants were allowed to practise their faith and to live freely. Hussain tells the story of one of the migrant Muslims, Ramlah, who divorced her husband because he converted to Christianity; and, continues Hussain, the husband died soon after converting because 'he had given himself over to frequenting wine merchants and consuming alcohol'. Later in the story, Muhammad wrote to Negus, as he wrote to many kings and rulers, inviting him to convert to Islam. Mention was made in Muhammad's letter of a version of the story of Mary and the virgin birth, and Negus was invited by the Muslim prophet 'to listen and accept my advice'. Hussain asks his readers to note how the contents of this letter clearly indicate that 'the Prophet understood the religious claims of the people of Abyssinia and wanted to express to them that his mission was a continuation of the prophetic traditions which they had inherited'. I assume that Hussain is drawing our attention not only to Muhammad's grasp of 'Christian' scripture, but to the 'fact' that Islam subsumed such 'prophetic traditions' and so was the natural successor to Christianity – there was no conflict between the two, as the earlier Christian story simply becomes part of the later 'final' Islamic one, Muhammad being the 'seal of the prophets'. The story continues with Emperor Negus writing back to Muhammad, commenting on the reference to Jesus and Mary, and pledging to surrender himself 'to the Lord of the worlds'. Later, Negus sends seven priests and five monks to Muhammad at Medina, where the Qur'an was read to them and 'they accepted Islam and wept and they were humble'.

Hussain's interspersed commentary on this story shows, to his satisfaction at least, that it can illuminate the contemporary *hijrah* of the Muslim community in Britain. The initial one-way relationship between Mecca and Abyssinia (when the Muslim migrants were clearly the suppliants) is replaced by the 'two-way' relationship between Abyssinia and Medina 'in so far as there were no restrictions on travel'. Muhammad is corresponding on equal terms (at least!) with the Abyssinian emperor, and indeed it is through Negus that he later asks for the hand in marriage of the widow Ramlah. When Negus dies, it is Muhammad who 'announces' his death. It is the liberal and tolerant Negus who is expected to convert (or assumed to have converted – the story as presented is unclear) to Islam: there is little thought given to the possibility that the Muslim asylum seekers might have something to learn from the Abyssinians.

There are, inevitably, various versions of this story of the Muslims who sought asylum in Abyssinia in 'the fifth year of the Prophet's mission', but the details do not really matter; what is remarkable is the telling of the story in the first place, a telling that (to make the point again) claims to offer a model for the 'proper' relationship between the British state and people and those Muslims currently resident here.

One quite clear message or moral of the story, *as told* by this modern student, is that the country (Abyssinia) to which, in 615 CE, this small band of persecuted Muslims fled was, in fact, as much in need of them as they were of it – an extraordinary claim, made even more extraordinary when seventh-century Abyssinia is offered as an exemplary model for Muslim arrival and settlement in Britain, a latter-day Abyssinia as it were. So, for example, Hussain refers to the various challenges facing the Muslims in Abyssinia and the Muslims in Britain. In Britain, he says, there is often a language barrier between Muslim parents and children, when children do not speak the mother tongue; and 'lack of opportunities in education, employment, and racism have given rise to frustrations and acts such as riots in some inner city Muslim communities' (Seddon *et al.*, 2003: 33). At that time of the Abyssinian exodus, Muslims were, in their own lands, a small, persecuted minority, unable to practise their religion, and persecuted by the Meccans: and yet into both contexts Muslims seem determined to import, along with themselves, a firm belief in the propriety of complaining about their hosts.

In what is, almost in its innocence, a rather amazing commentary, Hussain urges his readers to use the Abyssinian example as a corrective to the tendency for Muslim communities in Britain to become 'inward looking and [to create] a barrier between themselves and the wider community'. The Abyssinian example, he says, shows that Muslims are not inward looking; they were loyal to Negus and accepted him as sovereign – 'this is proved by the fact that the Prophet addressed him as "Negus the Stately or Great Ruler of Abyssinia"'. There was 'good will' between the Muslim and 'non-Muslim' communities because (in Christian Abyssinia at least) there was religious freedom and 'this resulted in a mutual respect which bore fruit when a two-way relationship between Abyssinia and the Muslim State in Madinah developed'. Hussain says that Islam 'oils the wheels of social cohesion and community unity', and

> the concept of *hijrah* inculcates a 'time and space' contextualisation of its teachings and endorses a redefinition of specific cultural practices and a new understanding of faith within contemporary settings and environments. Muslims should also endeavour to become positive role models. British Muslims should draw on the experiences of the early community that made *hijrah* to Abyssinia. They should realise that their *hijrah* is a natural process, which should instil them with confidence, and which will assist them in fulfilling their obligations to their Creator in this world. Finally, it is well known that the Prophet Muhammad declared that migration would not stop until the sun rises from the west (i.e. until the Last Day).
>
> Seddon *et al.*, 2003: 33–34

In 1888, Mohandas Gandhi was about to leave for England. News of this got about in Bombay, and he was summoned to a Hindu caste meeting, at which he was told that his proposal to go to England was 'improper, our religion forbids voyages abroad, one is obliged there to eat and drink with Europeans! It is not possible to keep our religion there!' (Gandhi, 2006: 24). Such an attitude is not to be found in Islam. The Muslim calendar starts with the earliest migration – the *hijrah* – and the stories symbolised by the calendar provide Muslims with a legitimation of foreign settlement, a confidence (arrogance even) in carrying it out, and a set of principles by which to implement *da'wah*, the purpose of *hijrah*. The stories, whether of Abyssinia 1,400 years ago or of the Crusades 1,000 years ago, or of the invasions of India (also 1,000 years ago), or of the occupation (and then, 500 years ago, the 'loss') of Andalusia, have a propagandist immediacy: they are not just stories. This latest version of the Abyssinia story is given to us, in 2003, by Imtiaz Ahmed

Hussain, at seminars held in 2002 in England, later published in a book containing a message from the then British home secretary, all aimed at explaining and justifying Muslim settlement in, and loyalty to, Great Britain! Hussain, in focusing on an event ('true' or not, it doesn't matter) that allegedly took place nearly 1,400 years ago – and in using this to derive a set of prescriptions for Muslim behaviour in Britain – perhaps gives away more than he realises. He confers virtue upon the emperor of Abyssinia, for example, by recounting the way in which the emperor seems to accept Islam, and the way in which he, the head of a major politically sophisticated state, treats as an equal the self-proclaimed leader of a small and precarious band of desert Arabs: Negus is approved of because (apparently) he became a Muslim, and because he accepted Muhammad as an equal! Hussain tells the story of Ramlah, who, enjoying the benefits of life in a tolerant Christian society, divorced her husband because he, exercising his freedom, became a Christian. The husband (naturally) goes on to become a drunkard; but 'the Prophet did not order the Muslims to leave Abyssinia in spite of this conversion to Christianity' – there is no sense here, in the story as told, that such a 'virtue' in the prophet might well be seen as an insult by Christians, in ancient Christian Abyssinia and perhaps even now.

Hussain insists in his commentaries that the Abyssinian story *proves* that Muslims can be loyal citizens in Britain – 'Perhaps the Muslim community does not have a problem with expressing its loyalty to the sovereign' – and then proceeds immediately to make this loyalty conditional upon some scruple (shared by many of us moderates) about the uses made by racist 'far right political groups' of our national symbols such as the Union Jack. Hence, 'they find it difficult to express their loyalty and belonging within such an exclusivist concept of what it means to be British'. This instant 'condition-making' is, of course, part and parcel of the endless *hijrah* that is Islam – as indeed we see, ironically enough, in Hussain's retelling of the story of Muslims in Abyssinia. We see Muslims enjoying the benefits of a free society – on condition, as Mr Ramlah found out, that the freedoms are not exercised! The conditions, the complaining, seem as migrant as the people. To be sure, Hussain does say that there are differences between Abyssinia and England, though little cheer can be had from his comments:

> Whereas the Muslims in Abyssinia looked towards the Prophet for guidance and inspiration, the Muslim community in Britain had to look toward each other and their links with their country of origin for moral and spiritual guidance. This reliance extended to the importing of spiritual leadership from their rural communities. This has resulted in these communities becoming inward looking and has created a barrier between themselves and the wider society. This barrier was an additional inhibitor which added to other barriers such as language and culture.
>
> Seddon *et al.*, 2003: 31

In the discussion that followed Hussain's paper, Zahid Parvez, of the University of Wolverhampton, thought that

> The 'identity crisis' experienced amongst young British Muslims of South Asian origin raises serious doubts about the concept and interpretation of 'integration'. What do we mean by this term? Are we suggesting subscription to a cultural monolith at the expense of all other social sub-cultures? The social exclusion of British Muslims, young and old, has had adverse effects on their 'loyalties' which are always viewed in absolute terms.
>
> *ibid.*: 36

As Emperor Negus may perhaps have mused, Muslims are hard to satisfy; and we can perhaps see only too clearly how long the list of conditions may be when we read the following, made in another contribution to Seddon's 2002 seminars. The director-general of the Islamic Foundation,

Dr Manazir Ahsan, writes that 'the Muslim community [is] unprotected due to the absence of a coherent set of laws on religious discrimination' (*ibid*.: vii). 'What', asks Dr Sayyid, of Salford University, 'is common to the experience of Muslims in Britain, apart from Islamophobia...and [being] commonly subject to regulation and discrimination and other forms of social exclusion?' (*ibid*.: 91). To be sure, Dr Sayyid goes on to say that such treatment certainly varies (by class and educational attainment) within the Muslim community, and that other 'ethnically marked populations' also experience problems. He then (pp. 91–92) goes on to call for a struggle on a variety of

> key issues (Kashmir, Chechnya, de-colonisation of the British state, greater social and economic equality, etc.) so that Muslims (and non-Muslims) could recognise in these issues the interest and identity of the Muslim community. This would be a far greater guarantee of a Muslim presence in public affairs than would an increase in the number of Muslim 'representatives' in parliament or the media. It is not the presence of individual Muslims, but a distinct and independent Muslim voice that will guarantee for Muslims a position beyond Islamophobia.

In addition, says Dr Sayyid,

> the problem of Islamophobia is not likely to diminish until the problem of a pan-European identity is itself resolved...how would Europe change as a result of recognising the Muslim presence in its midst?... This means that the Muslim presence has to become more openly associated with a critique of a way of thinking which considers European values to be universal and intrinsically superior. In other words, the articulation of a distinct Muslim subjectivity cannot be separated from a deepening of the process of de-colonisation.
>
> *ibid*.: 92

Complaint is piled upon complaint, condition upon condition: and there is little sense that it is the incoming Muslims who should be changing, and doing so without demanding overall societal perfection in the country in which they are privileged to live. It is, of course, clear from the Abyssinian story who has to change – not the incoming asylum-seeking band of early Muslims, fugitive members of an apparently failing religious movement, but the emperor of what was at the time a great and liberal state.

Where Dr Sayyid and other contributors to the 2002 seminars were relatively tentative about such triumphalist ambition, a school book for Palestinian children (ironically funded by the European Union) is rather more emphatic:

Western civilization flourished, as is well known, as a consequence of the links of the West to Islamic culture, through Arab institutions in Spain, and in other Islamic countries where Muslim thinkers and philosophers took an interest in Greek philosophy... Western civilization, in both its branches – the Capitalist and the Communist – deprived man of his peace of mind, stability, when it turned material well-being into the exemplary goal...his money leading him nowhere, except to suicide...

There is no escape from a new civilization which will rise in the wake of this material progress and which will continue it and lift man to the highest spiritual life alongside material advancement... Is there a nation capable of fulfilling such a role? The Western world is incapable of fulfilling it... There is only one nation capable of discharging this task, and that is our nation... No one but we can carry aloft the flag of tomorrow's civilization.

We do not claim that the collapse of Western civilization and the transfer of the centre of civilization to us will happen in the next decade or two, even in 50 years, for the rise and fall of civilization follow natural processes, and even when the foundation of a fortress became cracked it still appears for a long time to be at the peak of its strength. Nevertheless, [Western civilization] has begun to collapse and to become a pile of debris... We awoke to a painful reality and to oppressive Imperialism, and we drove it out of some of our lands, and we are about to drive it out of the rest.

Palestinian textbook for children,
quoted in Israeli, 2003: 51

To conclude: we Europeans tend to be diffident about our history. We learn it (in some strange way, now) to understand why and how and where we went wrong and yet how, providentially, we have been relatively successful. Muslims seem to learn their history to learn whom to blame for the fact that they are in decline, and how to re-create their supremacy, how to avenge themselves for defeats which, in Western eyes, belong (sensibly enough) in the past. The Lebanese writer Amin Maalouf says that 'the sack of Jerusalem [was] the starting point of a millennial hostility between Islam and the West', and that

The Arab world cannot bring itself to consider the Crusades a mere episode in the bygone past... In a Muslim world under constant attack, it is impossible to prevent the emergence of a sense of persecution, [so] Mehmet Ali Agca, who tried to shoot the pope on 13 May 1981, expressed himself in these terms: *I have decided to kill John Paul II, supreme commander of the Crusades.*

Maalouf, 1984: iv and 265

The nostalgia is resentful and angry. The past is something to be vengefully restored, if only because, in the past, Muslims were everywhere in the ascendant. Muslims retain a monocultural view of history, in which the 'mono' is Islam. This reflects a very large ambition: as the Muslim intellectual Eqbal Ahmad puts it, 'nationalism proceeds to create boundaries where Islam is a faith without boundaries. It interferes with the universalism that is the Koranic commitment of Islam, it is a universal religion that will not be subject to drawn boundaries' (Ahmad, 2000: 5). We Westerners, of course, live within such national boundaries. The nation state, democratically constructed, liberal in style, is the object of our political loyalty, as we insist it should be for all who would settle here. If Eqbal Ahmad is correct, then it is precisely this nation state that Muslims find unacceptable. Perhaps it is because their own nation states are not models of the *genre*.

CHAPTER 4

A BIOGRAPHY OF CONTEMPORARY ISLAM

Western Muslims should be free from the cultural
baggage of the Indian subcontinent, or the political
burdens of the Arab world... The Quilliam Foundation
rejects foreign ideologies of Islamism and Jihadism as
aberrant readings of the Islamic tradition and are thus
irrelevant and defunct. We uphold Islam as a pluralistic,
diverse tradition that can heal the pathology of Islamist
extremism.

Quilliam Foundation, pre-launch
document and website (18 April 2008)

The authors of this statement are young and courageous
ex-Islamists who are determined to present themselves as main-
stream, Moderate Muslims. They clearly wish to be able to
travel 'free of baggage' – or at least with different baggage: they
named their foundation after William Quilliam, one of the first
Englishmen to convert to Islam and actively promote it. The
Foundation presents itself as consciously and deliberately
'British' and, by extension, 'European'. They are clearly not too
at ease with the 'cultural baggage of the Indian subcontinent'.
Pace their sensitivities, however, the proclaimed justification for
multiculturalism is that members of the minority cultures
coming into Britain and Europe bring with them, from their
own cultures and countries (where else?), virtues that will
enhance the stability and prosperity of the host society: why else
do we need them? It is, then, quite proper to try to offer some
evaluation of the cultures and societies – the pedigrees, if you
like – with which our newly arrived minorities come equipped.

The previous chapter of this book dealt with aspects of the general culture with which, in a variety of ways, Muslims are imbued or in which they are invited to locate themselves. I will now look at the particular nations from which those Muslims resident in Britain derive their culture and identity. I am perfectly well aware that over half the Muslims currently resident in Britain were born here; but this is true of very, very few of their grandparents. Muslims (compared with me, for example) are new arrivals, deriving their political pedigree and moral inheritance from Muslim countries like Bangladesh and Pakistan. It is a perfectly valid question to ask: in which of these countries, if any, would a moderate British person like me feel able to live and bring up a family? Lest this automatically trigger the usual muttering of 'Islamophobia!' (or worse), may I call on Shaykh Abdal Hakim Murad (aka Tim Winter), who makes the point in exactly the same way. Shaykh Murad asked a 2002 conference: 'Muslims may be unhappy with the asylum laws here, but would anyone wish to claim asylum in any Muslim country that currently springs to mind?' He went on to suggest that, among other things, for example, criminal investigations of murder would be better dealt with in Great Britain than 'in, say, Iran or Saudi Arabia', and then to refer dismissively to 'ham-fisted attempts at creating Shariah states in several corners of the Muslim world' (Seddon et al., 2003: 20). Shaykh Murad is currently one of the five leaders of the international Muslim delegation that is involved in discussions with the Vatican. He is quite correct in identifying a considerable reluctance on the part of citizens of this country to migrate to countries under Muslim control.

Various bodies, in particular the UN, have, for some decades now, carried out evaluative social surveys of the 190 or so nations of the world (205 at the Beijing Olympics). These surveys have their limitations, of course. Some countries lack a formal system for collecting data; other countries have not been in existence long enough to figure in the statistical series for any length of time. This means that the data do not cover all countries in the same way on every measure. However, with that caveat, we do have more than enough information to provide us with an evidence-based assessment of the quality of life in all the different countries of the planet. We can compare the Muslim countries of the world with the other countries of the world. The United Nations has 193 member states, many (indeed most) 'new' since the end of the Second World War. There are 57 countries (and three 'observer' states) that are members of the Organisation of the Islamic Conference (hereafter OIC). I use the list of 57 as the basis for my calculations, although it has to be said that the inclusion of some of these countries on the OIC list is odd: are Nigeria, Mozambique or Uganda, for example, Muslim countries? Yet I have chosen to take the OIC list at face value. The statistical series presented below are all available on the web.

WELL-BEING: THE HUMAN DEVELOPMENT INDEX

The United Nations Human Development Index (HDI) aims to cover all the countries of the world, and to provide some kind of measurement to enable us to rank them in terms of 'well-being' or quality of life. This particular scale was developed by two economists, a Pakistani and an Indian, and measures things like life expectancy, literacy, education and general standards of 'well-being'. Other lists, such as UN documents on the least developed countries (LDCs), the Economic Vulnerability Index and data on low-income, food-deficit countries, also provide country-by-country data that enable us to locate the OIC countries within an assessment of the 'health and welfare' of the countries of the world. A comparison of OIC countries with all other countries is very illuminating, especially when related to the discussion in this chapter of the particular Muslim countries from which so many British-resident Muslims originate – not to mention the country to which they have chosen to migrate, the United Kingdom.

The UN Human Development Index is a standard means of measuring well-being, especially child welfare. The 175 countries on the index are divided into three categories: high, medium and low, where 'high' means the countries are doing well, and 'low' the opposite. Again, there are some problems with the lists and with the data. However, the index for 2007/08 (based on data for 2005) shows us that, whereas 47 per cent of the non-Muslim countries for which data are available score 'high', this is true of just 20 per cent of the countries on the OIC list of Muslim countries; 46 per cent of all non-Muslim countries appear in the 'medium' category, as compared with 55 per cent of the OIC countries; and 7 per cent of all the world's non-Muslim countries score 'low', as compared with 25 per cent of the OIC countries. Pakistan and Bangladesh, the main sources of the original (and continuing) immigration into Britain, are classified as 'medium'. The OIC countries for which data were not available included Afghanistan, Iraq and Somalia. Another UN 'ranking' system deals with the 50 'least developed countries' (LDCs) and uses criteria such as low per capita income and human resource weakness (poor nutrition, health, education). The Economic Vulnerability Index (EVI) measures things like an unstable agricultural sector, or instability in the export capability of each country. Of the 50 countries currently (2008) classified as LDCs, 20 (40 per cent) appear on the OIC list. Put another way, of the 57 OIC countries, 12 (21 per cent) are on the LDC list. Bangladesh, a major source of Muslim migration to the UK, is on this list. The UN also produces, through its Food and Agriculture Organization, lists of low-income, food-deficit Countries (LIFDCs). The figures for 2006 show that, of the 82 countries classified as LIFDCs, 36 (44 per cent) appear on the OIC list, among them Pakistan and Bangladesh. These two countries also appear on the various UN publications devoted to malnutrition, child mortality and education. In these tables, for example, Pakistan shows (for 2002) a 'calorie per day per person' score of 2,430 (an improvement of 130 over 1992); the figure for Bangladesh is 2,190 (an improvement of 120 over 1992). Bangladesh had a literacy rate of 50 per cent in 2002 (1992 – 42 per cent), and Pakistan had a rate of 60 per cent (1992 – 47 per cent). The UN literacy data do not separate males from females (an important issue considering the large-scale importation of brides from predominantly rural Pakistan and Bangladesh), but alternative data are available – see below.

The UK lies 16th on the Human Development Index, between Austria and Belgium. Bangladesh lies 140th and Pakistan 135th – both near the bottom end of the 'medium' category.

LIBERTY: DATA FROM (1) PRESS FREEDOM INDEX, (2) CAPITAL PUNISHMENT WORLDWIDE, AND (3) *OBSERVER* HUMAN RIGHTS INDEX

Another measure of the quality of life in a country is the Press Freedom Index, produced by Reporters without Borders. This index is based on the presence or absence of independent media, or the daily persecution and/or censoring of journalists. The index identifies those countries where there is no freedom of information and/or where the safety of journalists is not guaranteed. I have the 2004 index, which, not surprisingly, has Iraq as the most dangerous place for journalists. This index presents data for 167 countries. Of the 57 OIC countries, only one (Benin, which is in fact about 25 per cent Muslim) is in the first (best) quartile of the index, while another seven are in the second quartile. The third quartile accounts for 19, and 24 are in the last (worst) quartile. These include such major Muslim countries as Sudan, Pakistan, Bangladesh, Libya, Syria, Iran and Saudi Arabia. In the case of Bangladesh (ranked 151st), the authors draw attention to 'incessant violence. The government is partly to blame...but political groups as well as organised crime also persecute journalists.' Speaking of Pakistan, ranked 150th out of 167, the index says that 'the Army has sealed off the tribal areas [and there] has been increased army pressure on the local press'. Iran, say the authors, 'is the Middle East's biggest prison for the press', while in Saudi Arabia (159th), Syria (155th) and Libya (154th) 'the emergence of a free and independent press remains a mirage'.

MSN Encarta provides a table on capital punishment worldwide. From these data we see that 61 per cent of the countries of the OIC retain capital punishment, 16 per cent do not have it at all, and 23 per cent have it for restricted purposes and/or have not used it for at least 10 years. As for the 138 other countries, 29 per cent have capital punishment, 57 per cent do not, and 14 per cent fall into that last category of countries that have capital punishment for restricted purposes or where no capital punishment has taken place for at least the last 10 years.

The *Observer* Human Rights Index (OHRI) ranks countries according to 10 'headline abuses', and uses the HDI to give double scores to three of these (extra-judicial executions, disappearances, torture/inhuman treatment) so as to impose severer censure upon wealthy or wealthier countries which, the compilers revealingly say, 'should know better'. As a section of the Muslim world is quite wealthy – Qatar has the highest per capita income in the world, and Saudi Arabia is not far behind – this comment applies as much to them as it does to the more obviously wealthy countries of the West. The US Department of State is required to submit annually to the US Congress detailed reports on (in effect) all the countries of the world, and the OHRI makes use of these very detailed documents, as well as other reports from Amnesty International. The OHRI places 41 per cent of the OIC countries in the worst quartile of human rights abusers, 31 per cent in the second quartile, 27 per cent in the third quartile, and none in the last and best (or least offensive) quartile. Of the 135 non-Muslim countries, 16 per cent appear in the worst quartile, 22 per cent and 24 per cent in the middle two, and 38 per cent in the last and best category. Muslim countries on the OIC list account for 36 of the 100 'worst offenders' on the OHRI.

Slavery was abolished in 1962 in Saudi Arabia, and in 1970 in Yemen and Oman. Mauritania abolished slavery in 1980, but its own government states that it is alive and well (Bostom, 2005: 92). The dates on their own tell a large part of the story. Even Clarence-Smith, in a book on Muslim slaving activity (a book that is determined to put a pro-Muslim slant on the data), says that Muslim 'gradualism' (i.e. opposition and reluctance) in the anti-slavery campaigns denied Islam a pioneering role in the unfolding of a global idea of social freedom. Leaving infidels to determine the timing of abolition allowed for the theoretical possibility of a return to slavery… Reuben Levy is probably overly optimistic in thinking that victory [over slavery] had been achieved by the 1950s, for examples of slaves holding, and belief in the legitimacy of slavery abounded in that decade. The 1960s probably constituted the true watershed, when an Islamic accord against slavery triumphed, hastened by secularist agitation, and mainly informed by the cautious gradualism of Amir 'Ali.

Clarence-Smith, 2006: 218–21

Scarcely a ringing endorsement. On 19 April 2008, *The Times* reported on the case brought by a former slave, Hadijatou Mani, who took the government of her country, Niger, to the West African Community Court of Justice for failing to implement its own laws, which had criminalised slavery in 2003 (note the date). Ms Mani had been sold for £250 when she was aged 12: 'I have not had a day off in all my life, and I want this suffering of so many women to stop.' If she wins, then all 15 West African states will have to take action against slavery – something all of them have failed to do: there are thought to be about 43,000 people enslaved in Niger. The president of Timidria, the anti-slavery movement in Niger, claimed in 2004 that there were 870,000 slaves in Niger (out of a total population of 12 million), and said that 'slavery is a reality and current phenomenon, alive today at the start of the 21st century' (Anti-Slavery International website, accessed 7 June 2008).

These data reveal a Muslim world (and, of course, many other countries) in which liberal democratic ways of life are but fragilely established, if at all. Frederic Pryor concludes, from a wealth of data, that 'the greater the percentage of Muslims in [a] population, the lower are the political rights in the country…the general conclusion [is] that Islam has a negative impact on political rights' (Pryor, 2007: 2). Brian Barry agrees: 'No polity with a Muslim majority has ever given rise to a stable liberal democratic state' (Barry, 2006: 27).

The UK ranks 28th on the Press Freedom Index, equal with El Salvador and Hungary, and between Benin and the Dominican Republic. The authors of the Press Freedom Index state that 'the greatest press freedom is found in northern Europe (Denmark, Finland, Ireland, Iceland, the Netherlands and Norway), which is a haven of peace for journalists'. Of the top 20 countries, only three (New Zealand (9th), Trinidad and Tobago (11th) and Canada (18th)) are outside Europe.

The UK does not have capital punishment, and it appears in the third quartile of the OHRI, ranked 127th out of 195.

EDUCATION: PROFESSOR PERVEZ HOODBHOY

Professor Pervez Hoodbhoy provides figures for science and higher education in the Muslim world (Hoodbhoy, 2007). He is professor of physics at Quaid-i-Azam University in Pakistan. Like me, he uses the OIC list as a basis for comparing Muslim and non-Muslim countries. His article begins by asking: 'With well over a billion Muslims and extensive material resources, why is the Islamic world disengaged from science and the process of creating new knowledge?' Professor Hoodbhoy comments that Islam's Golden Age is now seven centuries in the past, and says that 'no major invention or discovery has emerged from the Muslim world for well over seven centuries'. In an analysis of physics and other scientific papers produced between 1997 and 2007, he shows that very few came from the seven scientifically most productive Muslim countries (Malaysia, Pakistan, Saudi Arabia, Morocco, Iran, Egypt, Turkey): Pakistan, for example, produced 846 physics papers, India 26,241 and the USA 201,062. Forty-six Muslim countries produced 1.17 per cent of the world's scientific literature. In all, OIC countries had an average of 8.5 scientists, engineers and technicians per 1,000 of the population, as compared to a world average of 40.7 and an average of 139.3 in the OECD countries. Such academic journals as do exist in OIC countries are poorly edited, badly refereed, and show signs of double-publishing and plagiarism. OIC research and development budgets average 0.3 per cent of GNP, as compared to a world average of 2.4 per cent. While the OIC countries are increasing these budgets, they lack sufficient engineers to make efficient use of the additional money: OIC countries have 400–500 engineers per million people, as compared to 3,500–4,000 per million in the OECD countries. Patents are negligible in the OIC countries – Pakistan, for example, has taken out eight in the last 43 years. Of the 1,800 OIC universities, only 312 publish journals; and no OIC country has a university in the top 500 universities index produced by Jiao Tong University, Shanghai. OIC incomes are only just below the world average; yet, according to a 2002 UN Muslim-authored report quoted by Professor Hoodbhoy, the translation of books into the languages spoken in the Arab world is, at 330 a year, at a level one-fifth that of modern Greece. He quotes the same report as saying that, in the 1,000 years since Caliph Maa'mun, Arabs have in total translated as many books as Spain now does in a single year!

Professor Hoodbhoy says that 'as intolerance and militancy sweep across the Muslim world, personal and academic freedoms diminish with the rising pressure to conform'. While women do have access to higher education, they are, on occasion, the recipients of such cheering messages as this one, which he quotes, from the head of a government-funded mosque-seminary:

> The government should abolish co-education. Quaid i Azam University has become a brothel. Its female professors and students roam in objectionable dresses... Sportswomen are spreading nudity. I warn the sportswomen of Islamabad to stop participating in sports... Our female students have not issued the threat of throwing acid on the uncovered face of women. However, such a threat could be used for creating the fear of Islam among sinful women. There is no harm in it. There are far more horrible punishments in the hereafter for such women.
>
> Hoodbhoy, 2007: 52

Professor Hoodbhoy comments that he and his colleagues have noticed how, over the years, such pressures reduce women to the level of 'silent note-takers, increasingly timid and less inclined to ask questions or take part in discussions'. Hoodbhoy has taught physics at the University of Quaid-i-Azam for 35 years. He says that his university has three mosques and a fourth one planned – but no bookshop. He would, without doubt, agree with Alasdair MacIntyre that 'No modern society in the West could have survived, could have maintained both its democratic forms and its rate of technical advance, and its flow of information and its communications, unless it had been prepared to accept the liberalization of intellectual life' (MacIntyre, 1967: 45).

WORK: THE GLOBAL COMPETITIVENESS INDEX

The World Economic Forum produces the Global Competitiveness Index, which, for 2007/08, ranked 131 countries in terms of how productively they used available resources. Of the 37 countries that appear on the OIC list of Muslim states and for which the World Economic Forum had useful data, 14 ranked at or above the mid-point, while 23 were below. Of the 37, four (Malaysia, Kuwait, Qatar and Tunisia) were in the first quartile, 11 were in the second, six were in the third and 16 were in the last quartile. In the case of Bangladesh, which ranked 107th out of the full list of 131, the report singled out corruption as the single main cause of its low standing. As for Pakistan, which ranked 92nd, corruption was compounded with poor infrastructure, inefficient government bureaucracy, political instability and an inadequately educated workforce.

The UK lies 9th on the Global Competitive Index, between Japan and the Netherlands.

HONESTY: THE INTERNATIONAL CORRUPTION PERCEPTIONS INDEX

This index is produced by Transparency International, 'a global civil society leading the fight against corruption. It is politically non-partisan and based on over 80 locally established national chapters and chapters-in-formation' (Transparency International website, accessed 27 August 2007). The index provides a 'corruption score' for the 180 countries for which it has data. The compilers regard a score of 5.0 as the borderline that distinguishes those countries that have serious corruption (below 5.0) from those that do not. Just three OIC countries are above that line – Qatar (6.0), the United Arab Emirates (5.7) and Malaysia (5.1) – while one (Bahrain) is at 5.0; all the rest are below, with 31 of them (54 per cent) at 2.0 or below. In 2005, Bangladesh (to which I return below) had the dubious distinction of being the world's most corrupt country for five years in a row – a record contested by the then government, but not so readily by the military government that took over and that was explicitly pledged (among other things) to rooting out corruption.

The UK ranks 13th on the International Corruption Perceptions Index, between Luxembourg and Hong Kong.

One of the small ironies of using these kinds of data is that they were originally meant, and are still generally intended by their authors and publishers, to illustrate the injustice of the world, and to provide exhortatory material for various kinds of redistributive international measures. Often enough, the articulation of these measures is accompanied by strictures on the rapacity of Western nations, whose relative success and self-aggrandisement has caused (so it is said or implied) the degradation of the rest of the world. The Muslim online magazine *Minaret* (published by the Institute of Objective Studies (*sic*)) adds a subtle and very typical Muslim twist to all this: that the West may well be financially and militarily successful, but it is culturally and socially worm-ridden, rotting from within through decadence and hedonism, 'compulsive consumerism and hedonism...the falling apart and decomposing of human relationships' (IOS *Minaret* website, April 2008). The West can be saved, *Minaret* implies, only by the simple virtues of Muhammad and Islam: echoes here of the cleansing competence of the pure desert warriors of Islamic legend, coming to save and liberate, not to conquer or oppress.

Having said all that, it is clear that the Muslim world is not very impressive; and, given the fact that they migrate from Muslim lands into the degraded and decadent West, many Muslims would seem to agree with this. Few go the other way. What for?

Migration into Great Britain is not random. There are at least 15 large (or largish) self-defining ethno-national Muslim communities in Britain (iCoCo, 2008: 2). Many, if not most, of the Muslims living in Britain have a Bangladeshi or Pakistani heritage. Nor is migration from those two countries random: most migration from Bangladesh comes from the province of Sylhet; in the case of Pakistan, it is from the region of Mirpur. Neither is migration from Mirpur and Sylhet random: sub-areas and even certain villages within Mirpur and Sylhet send their sons and daughters abroad. Undoubtedly, most Mirpuri Pakistanis and most Sylheti Bangladeshis are decent and nice people; but they migrate here from countries *to which* (quite frankly) one would not wish to emigrate. The data below come from a variety of sources, including those cited above, supplemented by other websites such as the Fact Files of the CIA, the bulletins of the International Crisis Group (ICG) and the routine reports made by the US Department of State to the US Congress.

BANGLADESH

It is from Bangladesh that many Muslims come to the United Kingdom. Most Bangladeshi Muslims come from the state of Sylhet, once part of the British-administered state of Assam. Islam is the state religion of Bangladesh. Sylhetis tend to congregate in London, their lives chronicled by (among others, and accurately or not) Monica Ali in *Brick Lane* and Ed Husain in *The Islamist*. Bangladesh, born through war in 1971, is 98 per cent Bengali and 83 per cent Muslim. In Bangladesh, life expectancy at birth for men and women is 63 years. Some 63 per cent of the labour force is engaged in agriculture, which accounts for only 19 per cent of GDP by value. The median age is 22.5; the population grows at 2.1 per cent a year, with 3.1 births per woman. Per capita income is estimated at $1,400. Nearly half of the population lives below the poverty line. Female literacy is 32 per cent, male 54 per cent. The land is the subject of regular and radical flooding, creating landlessness and the associated occupation and farming of low-yield, unhealthy lands. For these and other reasons, Bangladeshis are major 'self-exporters', whose remittances from the Middle East and Malaysia, as well as from the UK, amount to over $5 billion – equal to about half of Bangladesh government expenditure. Sylhet owes its comparative wealth to such remittances. They derive from Sylheti devotion to the catering business: it is said that 90 per cent of so-called 'Indian' restaurants are, in fact, Sylheti-Bangladeshi. Muslim Bangladesh owes its existence to a successful war with what was West Pakistan (also Muslim), and it has a large volunteer army that is able to draw on a reservoir of over 27 million men of military age. At present, the country has a military government; and, like Pakistan, it has cross-border conflicts involving irredentist 'terrorist' movements from the neighbouring or nearby Indian states of Tripura, Nagaland and Mizoram. These Indian movements allegedly obtain sanctuary and bases in Bangladesh by bribing Bangladeshi officials. As is the case with India and Pakistan, the Bangladeshi army deploys much of its resources to deal with internal security matters. The US Department of State's 2007 report on human rights practices says of Bangladesh that the security forces in Bangladesh 'frequently acted independently of government authority'; that, under the Emergency Powers Rules, freedom of association and freedom of the press were drastically curtailed; that, while the number of 'extra-judicial killings' by the security forces in 2007 was down on the previous year, there were still serious abuses, including about eight such killings a month (plus custodial deaths, arbitrary arrest and detention), with the security forces acting with impunity and going unpunished, even on the rare occasions when there was an inquiry into such deaths. Some 108 people were killed by 'vigilantes', with people taking the law into their own hands. The 108 could not represent the total number of people killed in this way, proper records rather inevitably not being fully available. Further, there were 234 reported kidnappings and more than 120 killings as a result of cross-border incursions by the Indian Border Security Force. Violence against women and children remained a major problem, as did people-trafficking.

A Transparency International report on Bangladesh says:

> Exchanges of money/gift and privileges are present and deep-rooted in the traditional culture of Bangladesh as is the case with many traditional societies across the world...in private sector gift-giving is pervasive and nepotism is normal...the causes of a secular increase in corruption i.e. related to cronyism, connections, activities of family members and relatives, political donations and bureaucratic deviation along with oversight of fraud and extra legal activities.
>
> Ahmad, 2007

It was, of course, in part these conditions that prompted a military takeover, the military leadership bent on cleaning up what seems to have become a seriously corrupt country. In its first year, the military government has made 444,000 arrests, prompting the International Crisis Group to say that 'there is now fear that the government is undermining the very democratic institutions it set out to rescue...creating a climate of fear in the country' (ICG, 2008).

PAKISTAN

Over half of the Muslims who live in Britain are of Pakistani origin. Pakistan is 97 per cent Muslim. It is an Islamic state. It has a male–female ratio of 52:48, and a female literacy rate of 32 per cent (male 55 per cent). Life expectancy at birth for men is 63, and for women 65. Pakistanis are young: the median age is 21, and there is an average of 3.71 births per woman. The per capita income is estimated at $2,600, and, while agriculture accounts for 20 per cent of the GDP by value, it employs 42 per cent of the labour force – a ratio that is almost inevitably a predictor of low agricultural standards of living. Roughly half of Pakistanis are Punjabis. At the time of writing, Pakistan has some version of a civilian government, but for most of its turbulent existence has been ruled by the army, which dominates Pakistan's economy, as well as its politics. Pakistan's army recruits primarily from the old British army recruiting area – the Punjab, of which Mirpur (while one of British India's 'princely states') was geographically part. The army of Pakistan is as much a Punjabi as a Pakistani army. With its various paramilitary cohorts, the army of Pakistan is about 10 times the size of the British army. It is engaged in a long-running on-off civil war with its own 'tribals', the Waziris, Pathans and Baluchis, and in cross-border involvement with the fighting in Afghanistan. Much of this conflict involves the growing (on both sides of the border) and smuggling of opium. The army's major military posture still assumes enmity and war with India, against which its major weaponry (including nuclear weapons) is deployed.

The Pakistani army, through a series of veterans' organisations and 'trusts', operates businesses in sugar mills, energy, fertilisers, cereals, cement, real estate, travel agencies, rice mills, fish farms and insurance companies. Transparency International's 2006 report on Pakistan shows very clearly indeed how all this meshes into a country in which, as a young woman told the BBC, 'Terrorism is a huge problem...but the country is enmeshed in corruption' (BBC, 2007). Transparency International's report on Pakistan refers to a widespread feeling among Pakistanis that corruption is endemic in matters connected with the police, the judiciary, land and taxation, customs, education, health and railways (see Transparency International, 2006). The US State Department, in its annual report to Congress in 2007, referred to considerable problems under the quasi-military rule of President Musharraf, who arrested 6,000 lawyers and under whom the security services engaged in a variety of killings, with little in the way of redress or punishment. The US State Department reported at least 1,550 cases of trafficking, over 1,600 'disappeared' persons, and widespread child abuse (bonded labour and outright sale). In Pushtun areas, there was the 'sale of girls as young as 11 as acts of retribution and to settle scores between tribes'. The Pakistani security forces were engaged in activities and assassinations against Baluchi and Waziris, who in turn attacked them, and there were major incidents at the Red Mosque (over 100 dead), Sunni–Shia disputes (a death toll of 300 in the district of Parachinar), and persecutions of Hindus, Ahmadis and Christians for 'desecrating the Qur'an', within a penal code that provides for the death sentence for those 'blaspheming' Muhammad. Yahya Birt writes that Pakistan has a serious heroin addiction problem, with the number of addicts going from zero in 1979 to 650,000 in 1986, 3 million in 1992 and 5 million by 1999 (Birt, 2001: 2). For all its wonderful people and its scenery, Pakistan is a good place not to be.

CHAPTER 5

SETTLING IN: CIVIL SOCIETY, SOCIAL NETWORKS AND TERROR

SETTLING IN?

Clearly, in-migrating Muslims do not simply transplant into Great Britain the full forms of social life in Bangladesh/Sylhet or Pakistan/Mirpur; indeed, they might, not surprisingly, be emigrating in order to get *away* from them. Equally clearly, they do not simply abandon their nationality or religion or ethnicity and overnight become British like me; indeed, they might find such a metamorphosis something to be resolutely resisted. What actually happens to 'our' immigrants? What can we expect of them? When we read accounts of what life is like in, say, Bangladesh or Pakistan, what do we think we have in common with them, or they with us? We now have many volumes of empirical studies of both Pakistanis and Bangladeshis. From these – and from once-despised common-sense truisms (truisms being, of course, true) – we can make an assessment of the compatibility, or otherwise, of our way of life with that of our new guests – and 'new' or 'foreign' (my major point, see below) is what they are. 'Foreign' is perhaps too weak a word, implying merely a negativity; something that is simply what we are not. As the above descriptions of Muslim states and countries demonstrate, our incoming settlers have some very distinctive and very real cultural attributes – though not ours.

Academic studies of these kinds of issues tend to be dominated by American accounts of the 'melting pot' – see, for example, the marvellous books by Thomas and Znaniecki on the Polish Peasant in Poland and America, or Irving Howe's more recent volume on Jewish migration-cum-flight from

Tsarist Russia to America. America is a nation of immigrants. We are not. We are a nation *with* immigrants. To try to cover such complexities, Robert Putnam has recently returned to a theme rather taken for granted by earlier writers: namely, that migration and settlement might well take time to assume their final and benign form. In the long term, he says, the coming of foreigners has economic and social benefit; but in the short term, in-migration 'reduces social solidarity and social capital...and trust (even in one's own race) is lower, altruism and communal co-operation rarer, and friends fewer' (Putnam, 2007: 137).

Putnam's underlying thesis assumes that there is a positive correlation between the level of integration and the length of settlement: the longer an incoming group is here the greater should be the level of integration – assimilation, even. For this to be anything but a platitude – who now cheers for the Anglo-Saxons? who now could spot a Pict? – the Putnam thesis must be able to show that each generation is on the path to more integration (or assimilation) than its predecessor: integration should proceed steadily, if not apace. While, as numerous studies show, this is not the case with Muslims resident in Britain, it is certainly true that the proponents of the various forms of multiculturalism would have us *believe* it to be true.

To begin with, integration is invented, *post facto*. Part of the effort *not* to integrate lies in the elaboration and reiteration of various invented pedigrees and genealogies. These 'genealogies' are paraded as fact, as if the 'fact' of an earlier presence was, on its own, proof of benign settlement and cheerful 'integration' (see Davies, 2007: 62–82). Their articulation seeks to assure us that Muslims, having been here for centuries, are a natural part and parcel of our way of life, no more and no less foreign than the Welsh or the Scots, familiar and co-developing, co-contributing, easily and constructively present now in large numbers: 'Muslim roots in British soil', says one official publication, before proceeding to put forward (as proof) an Arabic-inscribed coin, dating from the time of King Offa of Mercia, found in Ireland. This coin, stored in the British Museum, pops up very frequently in these 'pedigrees' – and is sometimes used to suggest that Offa was a Muslim. For example, mention of the coin occurs in a publication, *Muslims in Britain* (2004), a publication jointly sponsored (rather astonishingly) by the unlikely trio of the Foreign Office, the Home Office and the Muslim Council of Britain. This publication offers us a feature called 'Timeline Muslims in Britain', which, apart from the nugatory trivia of Offa's coin, tells us that in 1386 there were 'references to Islamic scholars in Canterbury Tales'. Neither this nor the ensuing parade of 'significant' dates ('1649: first English translation of the Qur'an') is any kind of plausible foundation for the claim that there are 'Muslim roots in British soil'. Muslims, along with other ethnic incomers, are very keen indeed to elongate the pedigree of their settlement, stretching it as far back as possible, thereby conferring upon themselves a share in the national story, a contribution to (and so a call upon) the national stock of wealth, security and culture. Furthermore, such pedigrees disarm any socio-political complaint about the alien 'newness' of their presence here: such a historical 'presence' creates the basis of a claim on the virtues of familiarity and an abatement of the possible vices of 'difference'. By claiming historical presence, they imply historical familiarity and they camouflage the very real differences between us. The more they are repeated, the more threadbare becomes the camouflage.

These pedigrees are spurious. As I said earlier, those Muslims who are genuinely able to impute descent from this putative British–Muslim gene pool would be very thin on the ground indeed. 'British' Bangladeshis and Pakistanis have been here in large numbers only since the 1970s/1980s. Of the 25,000 Muslims living in Britain in 1961, less than 2 per cent were born here. By 1971, there were 170,000 Muslims living here, of whom 24 per cent were born here; and by 1981 360,000, of whom 38 per cent were born here. The present scale of settlement, of something like 2 million, includes about 1 million Muslims born in Britain in and since the 1980s/1990s (Lewis, 1994: 15). These 'British Muslims' are new, not a population with a pedigree of Britishness. Further, and more importantly, and unlike Irving Howe's Jews, in-migrating Bangladeshis and Pakistanis are not here because they had to flee governmental hostility and pogroms in their native land. They are not asylum seekers. They migrated vol-untarily, and under conditions and at times more or less of their own choosing (the major obvious exception is that of the Ugandan Asians (including Muslims) evicted by Idi Amin (himself a Muslim)).

In addition (and again unlike the case of Irving Howe's Russian Jews), the countries from which they came (and come) remained and remain in existence, open for revisit and even return. These countries are permanent parts of the world of Muslim migrants to Britain and elsewhere; a world that is well equipped with the accoutrements and benefits of rapid global air and sea travel, websites and newspapers, banking and funding transactions, property dealing, religious recruit-ment of imams and money for mosque building, book pub-lishing and (crucially from the point of view of 'integration') the acquisition and importation of marriage partners for Pakistani and Bangladesh men and women – anxious, it seems, to retain rather than moderate their ethno-religious and linguistic separateness. Financial resources – and they are considerable – are available for things like mosque building and the publication and distribution of devotional and ideo-logical literature from the wide world of Muslim states, espe-cially the wealthy states of the Middle East. Furthermore, the 'tribal' areas and war-ready desert zones of North East Pakistan, Afghanistan and Sudan have provided many hun-dreds of young Muslim men born in Britain with a safe haven for ideological, military and weapons training. In such a con-text, how readily (even should they so wish) could Muslims from Pakistan and Bangladesh in fact shed 'the cultural bag-gage of the Indian subcontinent, or the political burdens of the Arab world' – the hope and aspiration held out by the recently formed 'counter-extremism think tank', the Quilliam Foundation? Thomas and Znaniecki's Poles and Irving Howe's Russian Jews had nowhere else to go, and nowhere to 'go back' to: they had to become American, and to work with what they had when they got off the boat in America. Their past was not only a different country; it was a country from which they were excluded. It was a country that no longer existed. Muslims are present in our country but absent from our history. Pakistanis and Bangladeshis are foreigners – literally, people from 'outside our door'. They are Muslims, also foreign. Mirpuri and Sylheti Muslims, decent folk though most of them certainly are, are foreign in ways in which Poles and Australians, West Indians and Americans, South Africans and Canadians, Italians and Norwegians are not. These comments are, to my mind, nothing but banality; yet to such depths has multiculturalism reduced our language that banality, like the small boy in the story of the Emperor's clothes, now expresses a dazzling truth: foreigners are foreign.

The newness of such Muslim incomers might explain why they do not really like us. A 2006 Pew Global Attitudes survey (Pew, 2006a) showed that 67 per cent of Muslims resident in Britain thought that the British were selfish, 64 per cent that we were arrogant, and 52 per cent that we were violent. Some 61 per cent of Muslims said that their relations with us Westerners were generally bad. Less than half felt that we were respectful of women. Only 32 per cent of Muslims had a favourable opinion of Jews, of whom, of course, 350,000 live in the UK – our home and their home for centuries. Heart-warmingly, the phlegmatic British do not return the insults: Pew polls state that 57 per cent of the British think that immigration from the Middle East and North Africa is a good thing. The figure was 61 per cent in 2005 and 53 per cent in 2002 – a remarkable level of goodwill, given the 2005 London bombings and other, persistent acts of violence. Some 81 per cent of Muslims living in Great Britain consider themselves Muslim before British. The most recent research on what is going on in Muslim society indicates that the 'horrific events of the 21st century, abroad and in Britain have had a profound effect on Muslims...precipitating a general withdrawal into their individual and ethnic groupings' (iCoCo, 2008: 22). There is less integration, it would seem, not more.

What else can we say about Mirpuris and Sylhetis, about Bangladeshis and Bengalis, Muslims all? While both Pakistan and Bangladesh have huge and growing cities, they are predominantly rural and agricultural – with all that that entails, not least (again!) that we and they are quite different: we are a highly urbanised society, and have been so for many generations. A report by Samad and Eade says that Muslim settlers in the UK are 'primarily rural in origin, working-class, low in human capital, and [with a] substantial young population' (Samad and Eade, 2002: iii). 'Working class' really means 'peasants', labourers on the land.

From the ratio of agricultural value to the size of the labour force in the GNP of both countries, as well as from figures on per capita incomes, we can deduce that Mirpuri and Sylheti immigrants will be poor. They are poor because they come from Pakistan or Bangladesh. They are not poor because they are here. Really poor Sylhetis and Mirpuris are those who stay in Bangladesh and Pakistan, where indeed the comparative wealth of those two provinces is due as much to remittances from abroad as to the hard work of the inhabitants. Both here and at home, there will be significant differences in the employment chances, literacy levels and health of men and of women: in both Sylhet and Mirpur the relationships between men and women are structured in ways that are foreign to us. Many of the brides 'imported' into the UK are young, illiterate (in their own language that is, never mind English), monolingual, and often cousins of their spouses: cousin marriage is commonplace. 'Young' means, among other things, that there will be a high birth rate; illiteracy means an extra educational handicap for children born into such a household; and cross-generational cousin marriages carry real health problems.

As is the case in most rural communities – for example, in Hindu India – marriages will be arranged (see below) and not left to the subtle perils of romantic love. Furthermore, as neither Mirpuris nor Sylhetis come from pluralistic multicultural societies, marriages will, if possible, be arranged within the bounds of ethnicity as well as of religion (see

Samad and Eade, 2002). There is virtually no marriage across the Muslim–British or Muslim–Christian lines of the UK. Moreover, ethnicity impels an inward-looking search for a marriage partner. The Silchar.com website asked: 'Would anyone agree that a marriage between a Sylheti and a Bengali would end up in a broken heart?' (Bear in mind that Sylhet is *in* Bengal/Bangladesh.) One respondent said: 'Many of us don't consider ourselves Bengalis, who are considered outsiders or foreigners by Sylhetis.' A Sylheti 'dating' or matrimonial site (Sylheti Matrimony) offers specific help for Sylhetis because the other 'Indian' matrimonial sites 'are available for Assamese, Kolkata Bengali, Gujarati, Hindi, Kannada, Kerala, Marathi, Marwadi, Parsi, Oriya, Punjabi, Sindhi, Tamil, Telugu, and Urdu'. (The site's office, interestingly enough, is in Assam, which practically borders Sylhet.) The languages the site lists are only the major languages; thousands more languages or dialects are spoken on the subcontinent. Clearly, marriage is assumed to be restricted to the particular ethno-linguistic group. Endogamous marriage takes place within groups determined to maintain their separate identity. Exogamous marriage is, *per contra*, a key indicator of cross-cultural integration.

There are several hundred thousand Sylhetis overseas: migration and remigration are well understood, well organised and legitimated by Islam. As is frequently the case (see, for example, Thomas and Znaniecki), religion, along with its various exclusivities, is often revitalised by migration, especially when both religion and migration are rooted in ethnic particularities. Decades and another continent ago, Thomas and Znaniecki noted how priests assumed a leading communal role in Polish communities translocated to America: religion became more important, not less, as a factor in identity formation. A report by Munira Mirza and others shows that the same mechanism operates with Muslims born in, and resident in, Britain. Of Muslims aged over 55, 71 per cent felt that they had as much in common with non-Muslims as they did with Muslims, while this was true of only 62 per cent of Muslims aged 16–24. The authors comment that 'the younger generation seems to be more "Arabised"...in adopting the religious habits, clothing and customs of Middle East Culture... The most striking expression of this is the shift to the growing prominence of Arab clothes for girls' (Mirza, 2007: 38–41). The iCoCo report already referred to also points to various trends among the younger generation that take them away from, rather than towards, greater 'integration'. It is interesting, too, that, in wishing to break away from 'unfettered ideology and its impact on adherents', the young(ish) Muslims engaged in setting up the Quilliam Foundation felt it necessary to reject 'the cultural baggage of the Indian subcontinent, or the political burdens of the Arab world'. These young men, once extremists, feel it necessary to try to 'become British' by distancing themselves from the dangerous pressures of the world and the Muslim *ummah* – but what they should move *towards* is somewhat less clear (see Chapter 8). None of this indicates a smooth progression, generation on generation, towards 'integration'.

In the case of Bangladeshis, Pakistanis and other Muslims, ethnic differences cut across religious commonality, which itself contains divisions. So the 'Muslim community' is, in fact, many communities, not one. While this intensifies intra-communal relationships and identities, it also reinforces inter-communal difference and mutual indifference rather than mutual friendship – after all, Muslim Bangladesh owes its existence to a very nasty war with Muslim Pakistan: a war fuelled by Bengali resentment of the pretensions to superiority and political dominance of West Pakistanis. Endless government attempts to summon up Muslim 'spokesmen' (generally men) are vitiated by the fissiparous and fractious nature of the 'Muslim community': there isn't one. There is no solid or common 'civil society' that can be characterised as 'British Islam'; no moderate majority; no representative, institutionalised common culture.

The iCoCo report says that there are at least 15 sizeable 'ethno-national Muslim communities in Britain, constituting probably the most diverse Muslim community in the world' (iCoCo, 2008: 2). The authors of the report refer to one of the least pleasant results of this diversity – the propensity of one ethno-national group to point the finger of 'extremism' at another, thereby diverting attention from itself (*ibid.*: 5). The corollary of that is, of course, a deep disinclination to point the finger at any member of one's own group. What we have now is not a steadily increasing integration, but a self-spawning (but government-sponsored) flurry of opinion and organisations – many clearly hostile to the West, some just as clearly seeking some form of *modus vivendi*, but generally on Muslim terms. The Quilliam Foundation, for example, seems to be unable to find in our purely British story any guide to its attempt to dissociate itself from 'Islamism'; instead it insists on looking for it (quaintly enough) in its 'Andalusian heritage', in medieval Baghdad, and in Indonesia! (According to the Barnabas Fund website (21 May 2008), Christians in Indonesia are currently being killed and are having their churches burned down by Muslim mobs.) It hardly needs me to point out (see below) that whatever virtues these societies possessed (and they are usually exaggerated), they were or are all Muslim dominated: even Moderate Muslims seem unable to escape the habit of command!

Perhaps this is because both Bangladesh and Pakistan are Islamic states – in the case of Pakistan, a semi-militarised Islamic state. No incomer from either country has any experience of being anything other than a member of a dominant and domineering state-enforced religion. 'Multiculturalism' in the UK is conferred upon them, not sought by them. It is not something they have practised at home. Minority religions in Pakistan and Bangladesh (and in other Muslim states) have a hard life. Furthermore, whereas, in most of Europe, religious life has been 'privatised' and secularised (see Chapter 6, and Barry, 2006), in most Muslim countries the opposite is true. Islam is heavily defended by the state in both Pakistan and Bangladesh: 'apostasy' or 'blaspheming Muhammad' carries the death penalty. In Pakistan, the law prescribes imprisonment or death for 'wilful defiling, damaging or desecration of the Holy Qur'an, and directly or indirectly, by words either spoken or written or by visible representation, or by an imputation, innuendo or insinuation defiling the name of the Holy Prophet' (Pipes, 1999: 4). While no one has, to date, suffered capital punishment, dozens are in prison awaiting trial. Christians and Hindus, as well as the unfortunate Ahmadis, incur much vigilante displeasure, with the police busy looking the other way. Islam is day-to-day ubiquitous in Pakistan and Bangladesh – and getting more so. It constantly erupts into political and national life, and indeed offers (though seldom delivers) the promise of political stability to failed or failing Muslim states like Pakistan and Bangladesh – and, indeed, Afghanistan. The sheer ambition of such a promise, failing a definitive and effective institutionalisation in actual state power, expresses itself as angry nostalgia and religious rodomontade, taking immediate and violent offence at 'blasphemies', jokes and satire. Indeed, when it comes to the prophet Muhammad, there is simply no satire available, no joke allowed. Sadly, this ludicrous sensitivity is now imported into Britain. Ben Elton, the comedian, says that the BBC refused to allow him to use the old saw about Muhammad and the mountain – 'the BBC will let vicar gags pass, but they would not let imam gags pass' (*Times*, 2 April 2008). Denmark, the home of 'incendiary' cartoons, is shortly to be blessed, and to have its joke-telling capacity reduced, by the arrival of Al-Azhar University courses, a development welcomed by the Islamic Faith Society and the Danish–Egyptian Dialogue Institute of Cairo (*Copenhagen Post*, 9 April 2008). Cartoons, novels, teddy bears – Muslim responses to these trivial things all indicate a level of immersion in a highly communalised but global religious affiliation that is very alien to even the religiously minded people (Christians) of Western Europe, let alone to Europe's numerous secularists, atheists, agnostics and humanists. The *Muslim Directory*, a major compendium on the commercial and cultural structures of the Muslim presence in Great Britain, offers the following advice:

Why does Islam often seem strange to non-Muslims?
Islam may seem exotic or even extreme in the modern world. Perhaps this is because religion does not

dominate everyday life in the West today, whereas Muslims have religion always uppermost in their minds and make no division between secular and sacred. They believe that the Divine Law, the Shar'iah, should be taken very seriously.

Muslim Directory, 2007/08: 550

Muslims may well be moderate; but in their origins and homelands they are very different from us, and they remain different from us when they settle among us. It is an open question whether 'moderate' is a term that can transcend that difference, and in so doing absolve these differences of being the source of antagonism. It surely has to be said at this point that lessons derived from anthropology, sociology and social psychology – not to mention our day-to-day experience – overwhelmingly indicate that radical cultural differences do not make an easy home for amicability and mutual trust.

Were Muslims to claim that their civil society spontaneously generates a capacity for such things, then we would have to ask why it is the *government* that is importing imams to offset troubles in the mosques and madrassahs; why it is the *government* that both creates and funds programmes that seek to encourage Muslim women to 'gentle' their men; and why now (*Muslim Weekly*, 18 May 2008) it is again the *government* that is setting up a 'Young Muslims' Consultative Group' to try to get young Muslims to see the sense of a constructive engagement with the British way of life. True, there is a problem with the behaviour of young Muslims – young men in particular.

THE MUSLIM CRIME WAVE: MUSLIMS, DRUGS AND THE CRIMINAL JUSTICE SYSTEM

We are, sadly, used to seeing Muslims and the police meeting each other only on the frontiers of terror. It comes as some relief to know that Muslims do, in fact, commit ordinary 'moderate' crimes; though it is somewhat alarming to learn that, though only about 2 per cent of the general population, they now constitute about 9 or 10 per cent of the prison population. We are living through a Muslim crime wave. In 2001/02, there were 4,445 Muslims in prison in England and Wales (Spalek, 2002: 7). Given the assumption that the Muslim population of England and Wales in 2001/02 was about 1.5 million (though it was probably nearer 1 million), the figure of 4,445 represents 0.3 per cent of the total Muslim population. If the general population of England and Wales (53 million) had the same crime rate as Muslims, then in that year the general prison population would have been nearer 150,000 than the 66,300 it in fact was. A similar calculation, for the same year, for Sikhs and Hindus (each at about 500,000 in the total population), would have placed 1,900 Sikhs and 1,900 Hindus in prison, when there were in fact 418 Sikhs in prison and 254 Hindus (*ibid.*).

The *Muslim Directory* goes on to paint a most distressing picture of the relationships between Muslims and the British criminal justice system – and, while fairly typically managing to either ignore or underplay both the crime wave and terrorism, also manages to impute Muslim criminality to the hostility and prejudice of the British state.

After describing the directory, which has a very wide circulation, I quote its 'analysis' of the Muslim crime problem in full: it is a most revealing and depressing diatribe. I then move to a discussion of the British Crime Survey to see what justification there might be (if any) for this persistent Muslim vilification of the British criminal justice system. Finally, I look at what is a rather hidden truth about Muslims living in Britain – the Muslim Crime Wave.

The *Muslim Directory* is a major compendium of the Muslim presence in Britain. Begun about 10 years ago, it claims an all-edition circulation of over a million (with 111,000 copies of the current edition). The 2007/08 edition is an extraordinary 700-page, thin-paper, closely printed publication, and is the type of book that is now quite unfamiliar to the Western secular mind. It is part canonical or liturgical text (it starts with several quotes from the Qur'an ('In the name of Allah, Most Gracious, Most Merciful')), part almanac, part trade directory, part political broadsheet, part encyclopaedia, part proclamatory proselytising. It offers explanations of the meaning of Muslim names and a monthly prayer calendar, lists and addresses of mosques and book-shops, charities, solicitors, accountants, funeral arrangers, Muslim schools, travel agents, department stores and dating or marriage guidance agencies. If anything, it is like the direc-tories once published by the Methodist Church, in which the business of buying and selling were all wrapped up in the urg-ings of Methodism, the latter being the guarantor of the pro-bity of the transactions of the former. The *Muslim Directory*, however, goes beyond that. In its introductory 'Publisher's Note', it provides us with a guide as to how it sees the posi-tion of Muslims in our country, and it is interesting to see how heavily the police and the criminal justice system weigh on the publisher's mind. I quote in full, merely commenting that what the authors regard as a quickly dismissed problem (Muslim terrorism) may perhaps be deserving of rather more extended treatment.

The Publisher's Note starts by saying: 'Though we had hoped and prayed that we would be able to write a more "up-beat" note from the last edition, the events that have taken place since have worried both us and the community.' It goes on:

> The community has always upheld the rule of law and will always denounce the warped individuals whose aim it is to hurt the whole of our society. We have been living in peace here for over 100 years and will continue to do so but recent events have ensured that Islam itself is now a target of institutions and individuals from all walks of life including the media and government.

The brief and dismissive reference to terrorism ('warped individuals') is immediately capped by the complaint about the way in which the community ('living in peace...for over 100 years') is now being targeted. This provides the refrain for a long paragraph that follows. This list of the assaults and injustices that are visited upon the Muslim community may be regarded as a version of what British civil society and the police look like to these influential Muslims. In what seems to me to be little more than a minatory diatribe, we learn of:

The continued stereotyping of Islam and its adherents; the incarceration and proposed extradition of British citizens to the USA including Babar Ahmad without any recourse to the British courts; the politicisation of public institutions, such as the police; the shooting and arrest of innocent Muslims; the arrest of Muslims whose 'sub judice' case details are actively leaked by the Police with the alleged involvement of the Home Office; the media 'frenzy' which is allegedly 'stoked up' by our government to side-track local and global issues; the release, without charge, of many of those arrested without the same scale of media reporting; the increase in Islamophobia and the refusal of public institutions such as the Metropolitan Police to acknowledge this; the active government withdrawal from liaising and consulting with main-stream Muslim organisations; the ridiculous and continued blame, demand and onus on the whole community by the government for it to 'prevent terrorism' yet at the same time actively alienating large quarters of the community; the systematic curtailment of our civil liberties; the arrest, imprisonment and solitary confinement of people for several years without charge in the UK and the obliteration of 'habeas corpus ad subjiciendum' and continued torture and inhumane detention of hundreds in Guantanamo; the extradition of individual Muslims to countries of torture and our governments (sic) compliance with the USA on rendition; the continuous demands led by our 'free and unbiased' media to ban and censor non-violent political organisations and some charities and criminalise certain opinions and the demand on the community to distance themselves from oppressed people around the world have greatly affected, concerned and worried us all as British

Muslims and what effect this will have on the future of our children in this country.

This air (storm?) of persecution is replicated in many editions of the English-language Muslim newspaper, the *Muslim Weekly*. On 8 February 2008, it proclaimed that 'Bugging Scandal Highlights Distrust' (of the police) and quoted M. A. Bari, secretary-general of the MCB, as saying that the alleged bugging of Sadiq Khan MP was 'simply appalling...[and] raise[s] a whole range of vital issues to do with confidentiality and how to hold to account the improper behaviour of senior police officers'. The *Muslim Weekly* went on to quote the chairman of the British Muslim Forum, Khurshid Ahmed, who said that the alleged bugging of Sadiq Khan MP, in discussion with one of his constituents in prison, would, if true, 'reinforce the fear and suspicion among the Muslim community'. Three years before, the same newspaper had reported that the London law firm of Dean and Dean was preparing a claim against the Metropolitan Police for discriminating against Muslims: Massoud Shadjareh, chairman of the Islamic Human Rights Commission (IHRC), said that 'the reality is that the Muslim community is being failed by police forces up and down the country' (*Muslim Weekly*, 18–24 March 2005). On 9 November 2007, Massoud Shadjareh appeared again in the *Muslim Weekly*, under a headline asserting that the 'Head of MI5 Exaggerates Terrorist Threat'. He claimed Europol figures showed that 'out of 498 terrorist attacks in 2006, only one was committed by a Muslim... We need to look at the reality and stop targeting specific communities.'

In response, I wrote to the *Muslim Weekly*:

Dear Editor

Please allow me to comment on your November 9 article based on the IHRC's reference to the head of MI5. The Europol Report to which he refers says, and I quote: 'Half of all terrorism arrests were related to Islamist terrorism: The frequency of video statements by members of the original al-Qaeda group and other

Islamist terrorists show a marked increase: [Of the 498 attacks in the EU in 2006] the vast majority resulted in limited material damage. However, the failed attack in Germany demonstrates that Islamist terrorists also aim at mass killings.'

You will have to believe me when I say that we all want a quiet life, that there is no devious or malicious plot to vilify or caricature Muslims: but you have to face up to the grim spectre that is arising out of your community. This argument about terror is not taking place about Hindus or Sikhs, or Jamaicans or Poles. It is not an invention of some lunatic determined to scapegoat and harass Muslims.

This letter was published in the next edition, but with no comment or response. Like many others, the *Muslim Weekly* and Mr Shadjareh prefer to go into a state of denial about EU-wide Islamist terrorism and its reporting. Neither of them, for example, mentioned that 257 of the 706 EU-wide terrorist arrests were Islamist-related (Europol, 2007: 4.2). They fail to mention that the data are often incomplete, national police forces (for obvious reasons) preferring to 'mask' their activities: the UK, for example, provides data on only a small number of 'high-profile cases' (*ibid.*: 3.2). Europol's 2008 report says that in Britain the figure for arrests for terror-related offences in 2007 was 30 per cent up on the previous year. Of 404 terror arrests in Europe, the UK accounted for 203. Britain is 'the focal point for Islamic terrorism across Europe' (Europol, 2008: 4.2) – in part, Professor David Capitanchik told the *Independent*, because 'we have such a large immigrant population which is more vulnerable to radical Islamic thinking' (*Independent*, 18 May 2008). Of course, had Mr Shadjareh, instead of looking at 2006, taken the figures for a year earlier, he would have found several Muslim bombers on London trains and buses.

As noted above, whether in articles or letters, in organs such as the *Muslim Directory* or the *Muslim Weekly*, leaders of the Muslim community seem determined to react with instant anger and threats to what they insist is systematic bias towards, and persecution of, their always innocent co-religionists. I have already referred to the truly astonishing 'promise' made by Dr Bari of the Muslim Council of Britain that, unless the police changed its ways, he could and would unleash 2 million Muslim terrorists onto the streets of Britain. I assume that Dr Bari genuinely and honestly sees in the behaviour of our police so consistent a bias against, hostility to and persecution of Muslims as would justify his slandering of the Muslim community (can they really all be turned so easily into terrorists?) and his issuing of such a threat to the entire British populace.

As it happens, the British Crime Survey seems to indicate that, as far as the police and the criminal justice system (CJS) are concerned, most members of all ethnic minorities, most of the time, have confidence in the CJS; and Muslims are among those least likely to be dissatisfied with the police and the CJS (see Home Office 1997; 2001a, b, c; 2003a, b; 2004; 2005; 2006a, b; 2007; 2008). The British Crime Survey reports every year on 'consumer' attitudes to the CJS (which generally includes the police). Respondents are divided into three groups: self-defined whites, self-defined Asians and self-defined blacks. Of these, over the six years in question (2001–07), self-defined whites and self-defined Asians reported a level of 'confidence in the way the CJS handled crime suspects' that, in percentage terms, was in the mid- to high-70s; meanwhile, the self-defined blacks recorded a confidence level in the mid-60s. On the question of 'confidence about meeting the needs of the victim of crime', self-defined Asians had the highest level of confidence in the CJS (an average over those years of 53 per cent); self-defined blacks had an average of 44 per cent; and self-defined whites an average of 32 per cent. For 2006/07 – that is, *after* the London bombings – self-defined Asians (76 per cent) were confident that the CJS 'met the need of crime suspects'; the figure for self-defined whites was 79 per cent. On the question of whether the CJS 'met the needs of crime victims', 53 per cent of self-defined Asians said it did, compared with 31 per cent of self-defined whites. For that same year, 56 per cent of self-defined Asians felt that the CJS was 'effective in reducing crime', as opposed to 34 per cent of self-defined whites. Of the self-defined Asians, for 2006/07, 76 per cent felt that the CJS 'respected the rights of suspects', while the figure for self-defined whites was 79 per cent. Lastly, 41 per cent of the self-defined Asians felt that the CJS was 'effective in dealing with young suspects', as compared with 23 per cent of self-defined whites. If anyone is aggrieved at the police and the criminal justice system, it is the whites!

The category 'Asians' is obviously not restricted to Muslims. A 2001 report (Home Office, 2001b) separates Pakistanis and Bangladeshis from Indians, treating the first two as one category. Though the sample size leaves something to be desired, there are indeed differences between the various religious or ethnic groups. In 1993, for example, Pakistanis plus Bangladeshis were nearly twice as likely as Indians (8.1 per cent, compared with 4.9 per cent) to be the victim of a racially motivated incident; but by 1999 the difference had been reduced, and the incidence for Pakistanis plus Bangladeshis had practically been halved – 4.2 per cent, compared with 3.6 per cent for Indians (*ibid.*: 23). There was, of course, a general reduction in official crime rates over those years.

'Overall', write the authors of the report, 'risks of personal crime were highest for black people... Risks for Indians, Pakistanis and Bangladeshis were broadly similar to those for white people' (*ibid.*: 11). Other data showed that, whereas in 1996 the percentage of victims who were 'very or fairly satisfied with Police response' was the same (52 per cent) for Indians, black people and Pakistanis and Bangladeshis, by the year 2000 Pakistanis and Bangladeshis, at 43 per cent, were expressing less satisfaction than black people (52 per cent), Indians (51 per cent) and whites (58 per cent). Of people who sought police contact, 63 per cent of Pakistanis and Bangladeshis expressed satisfaction, compared with 67 per cent of black people, 62 per cent of Indians and 72 per cent of white people (*ibid.*: 48–49). Jefferson and Walker's 1993 study of Leeds showed that Asians had more favourable attitudes towards, and fewer unpleasant experiences of, the police than was the case for either blacks or whites (Jefferson and Walker, 1993).

Such data do not support the repullulating level of denunciation made of our criminal justice system by so many Muslim 'representatives'. These vehement denunciations are perhaps made for two reasons: firstly, to mask the Muslim crime wave and secondly, to demand – and get – preferential treatment.

I repeat the point I made earlier: if the crime rate for the generality of the British population was the same as that for Muslims, then the prison population would be considerably higher than it is today. Yahya Birt, a 'revert' or convert to Islam, wrote in 2001 that:

> This surge in Muslim crime is not being discussed openly within the community...probably out of a sense of shame. But in reality we should feel ashamed because we are not facing these problems openly and discussing them.
>
> Birt, 2001

Birt goes on to point out that, at the time about which he wrote (2000/01), the 4,000–4,500 Muslims in prison were mostly (65 per cent) men between the ages of 18 and 30. Significantly, this did not include youngsters under 18 who were in various types of custodial institutions. He quotes Maqsood Ahmed, the Muslim adviser to the Prison Service, who said that over 1,000 of those Muslims in prison were there because of involvement in drug using and drug distribution. Birt also quotes Tower Hamlets Police, and Tower Hamlets Muslim activist Abdur Rahman, whose comments reinforce the picture of young Pakistani and Bangladeshi males active in both consuming and dealing in drugs, and in the formation of street gangs caught up in drug-related turf wars and other conflicts.

Marie Macey's (2002) examination of young male Muslim involvement in crime in Bradford supports this picture. The largest and fastest-growing minority in Bradford is from Pakistani Mirpur, and it is this Pakistani Muslim minority that accounts for by far the largest part of the national increase of South-East Asians in British prisons. Again, there are difficulties in relating statistics on religion to those on particular crimes, but Macey is quite clear that 'the only comment that can be made on these statistics with any level of confidence is that the majority of the illegal drug trade in Bradford is controlled by Pakistani Muslims' (Macey, 2002: 26). This should not surprise us. Yahya Birt tells us that:

> Muslim involvement in hard drugs is not confined to Muslims in the West. Of the traditional 'natural' drugs, Muslims are heavily involved with the planting, harvesting, refinement, smuggling and distribution to Europe of heroin and cannabis... Pakistan has the highest heroin addiction rate in the world... In 1979 [there were] no addicts...three million in 1992, while in 1999 government figures estimate a staggering figure of five million.
>
> Birt, 2001

Birt comments that 58 per cent of opiates are consumed in South Asia, the area of production, giving a rather different picture from the usual one of a drug-dependent West creating a demand for drugs that poverty-stricken Afghani subsistence farmers are 'forced' to satisfy.

Macey's figures for the prison population of England and Wales indicate that the *types* of crime committed by the three main ethnic groups are fairly evenly spread, though the figures for the relatively high rates of Asian involvement in crimes of violence against the person, as well as drug crime, fly, as she says, 'in the face of commonly held stereotypes of ethnic groups' (Macey, 2002: 25–26). She describes the style and nature of young Muslim men's involvement in the public disturbances in Bradford in 1995 and 2001, and from that analysis, and from her analysis of what she calls 'specifically Muslim crime', she concludes that, while such young men are a 'tiny minority of the Pakistani Muslim population in Bradford',

> Criminal and neo-criminal behaviour is having a massive negative impact on the city and, indeed, on wider society. In Bradford, they are significantly adding to the city's already high level of poverty in a number of ways – both social and material – that have harmful short- and long-term consequences. These include exacerbation of already high levels of ethnic division and tension; preventing young Muslim women from fulfilling their potential; 'driving out' young people from all ethnic groups (including white); increasing expenditure through policing bills and property repairs; and creating a negative image of the city that not only discourages inward investment and job creation, but is also causing established businesses to relocate. In terms of wider society, there is little doubt that the public disorders of 1995 and 2001 have exacerbated negative images of Islam in ways that could have long-term consequences for inter-ethnic and inter-faith relations.
>
> *ibid.*: 42

This description is almost the antithesis of that given us in the *Muslim Directory*: there, the agencies of the British state harass and persecute law-abiding Muslims; here, a gang of Muslim thugs and criminals harasses and destroys the stability and prosperity of an entire city.

To explain this Muslim crime wave, Dr Macey adduces (1) a perception on the part of those involved of some sort of religious requirement, (2) the influence of international Islam and the brotherhood of the *ummah*, (3) the politics of the Indian subcontinent, and (4) Mirpuri cultural traditions (*ibid.*: 27). This is, of course, a description of a community that is propelled by forces scarcely likely to see it well set on the road to 'integration'. It should be noted that such a congealing of a separate identity for Muslims divides them as much from other Asian communities (such as Sikhs and Hindus) as from whites. Such 'ethnic' or 'communal' politics, heavily 'gendered', is already resulting in conflict, electoral fraud and mutual distrust.

Three other things need to be said about Marie Macey's contribution to the topic of the current Muslim crime wave and its relationship with the drug business. First, she stands witness to the open attempts made to hide the truth of what is going on. One of her colleagues, in an academic seminar where she was giving a paper on London Bangladeshis, found herself in a 'highly charged debate', in which she was criticised for not concentrating on issues of racism. She then received the quite common *ad hominem* (*ad feminam?*) stricture that white women should not be researching Muslims anyway. Dr Macey goes on to tell how abuse and physical attacks on researchers and students have created a 'climate of fear and oppression [that] extends to research and scholarly pursuits'; her own students have been physically assaulted. The Ousley Report, which she quotes, dealt with the 2001 riots; it, too, pointed out that attacks and threats meant that, among other things, white Bradfordians – themselves neither rich nor prosperous – felt denied a voice, even though, in some areas of the city, over 70 per cent of racial assaults were on them. Denial of truth and euphemism are now the order of the day. Macey states that researchers face 'fear and oppression and the silencing of voices that suggest alternative analyses' (*ibid.*: 19–20).

Second, the depiction of the power and dominance of a criminal and violent minority – in this case, young Pakistani male criminals – over its own community should be borne in mind when considering the function, within other (doubtless moderate) Muslim communities, of that other (or over-lapping?) group of violent-minded young men we call 'terrorists'. Macey describes how, in the Bradford riots of 1995, the older Muslim men – 'elders, community leaders and councillors' – and women's groups were elbowed aside or simply ignored by young men newly discovering, in riot, their power to control and intimidate. Women, in particular, find in this violence a reminder, if they ever needed one, of their vulnerability (Macey, 1999). Neither terrorists nor criminals need to assemble in large battalions: they can freeze the righteous ones in society into fear and immobility. In such contexts, old saws carry real truths: 'all that is necessary for bad men to get their way is for good men to do nothing', or 'if you're not against them, then you're for them'.

Third, when we take together the writing of Marie Macey and Yahya Birt, we must, it seems to me, be very concerned indeed at the way in which official concessions made to Muslim sensibilities may all too often be concessions to a voluble and self-promoting minority, itself short on tolerance. Before moving on to a relatively short discussion of terrorism (short because it is well discussed elsewhere), I will make some brief comment on the way in which the criminal justice system has subverted itself in order to elicit the plaudits of the multiculturalists.

In 2005, a conference took place at the Regent's Park Islamic Centre. The Metropolitan Police and the Association of Chief Police Officers (ACPO) were sponsors of the event, along with three Muslim organisations. The uniformed ACPO representative introduced himself with an Arabic greeting (*salaam alekum*), told the gathering (400 or so Muslims, mostly men) that Islam was a great religion, which they (the police) did not understand; the recent London bombs were a great shock: the police service, he said, did not know the Muslim community, and he, though regarded as an ACPO expert on such matters, did not really know all that much either: 'We police around your communities, but not in them.' Some mosques, he said, had been berated by angry young men (with whom, frankly, he did 'not agree'), but 'having extreme views does not make you a criminal'. The police, he went on to say, needed the community to help them: the police pledged themselves to deal with Islamophobia and hate crime; the most important thing was that the police would protect Muslims in these difficult times, *inshallah*. Applause (author's own notes, 24 July 2005).

Well before this event, in 2000, 'some leading concerned Muslim organisation [*sic*] following 9/11 and the subsequent unfair [policing] focus on the Muslim community...had combined to create the Muslim Safety Forum' (Muslim Safety Forum (MSF) website, 28 April 2008). The forum, by its own account, came into being (in 2000) *before* the events of 11 September 2001 (9/11) – and yet it is 9/11 that, the MSF claims, called it into being. Whatever the truth of the matter, the MSF, ACPO and the Met seem to have found common cause in the proposal to create panels of Muslims, whom the police would consult *before* they mounted counter-terrorist raids. Such panels would offer an assessment of the information in the possession of the police, and would comment on how the Muslim community might react. Panel members would not be obliged to sign the Official Secrets Act. The proposal, in 2006, to establish such panels in all police areas seems to have run into opposition and would appear to be in operation only in London, although variants of it are appearing elsewhere. The Muslim Safety Forum now boasts that it is:

> the key advisory body for the Police Service...advising the police on matters of safety and security from the Muslim perspective. It meets on a monthly basis with senior representatives of ACPO and the Metropolitan Police service, the Metropolitan Police Authority, the Home Office and the Independent Police Complaints Commission amongst others... The overriding objective of the MSF is to identify the safety and security needs of the Muslim community of the UK...we are looking at activities within the policing service that can generate anti-Muslim feelings or disproportionate policing in the community...intelligence being opened up to selected independent community people who can provide oversight and advice on such materials before any operations are mounted.
>
> MSF website, 28 April 2008

Other police forces are experimenting with versions of this: Strathclyde's chief constable, for example, is in discussion with the recently formed Association of Muslim Police, which offers to advise senior staff on 'cultural and religious sensitivities'; meanwhile, the Northamptonshire force has set up the 'Northamptonshire Police Muslim Support Forum', Assistant Chief Constable Talbot saying that 'we are trying to engage more constructively with the Muslim community' (*Muslim Weekly*, 25 April 2008).

The Prison Service, too, is seeking more constructive engagement with the Muslim community. So, for example, we have Muslim sex offenders insisting on the right to opt out of treatment programmes intended to stop them reoffending, since open or public discussion of their crimes is, they argue, against their religion (*Times*, 9 April 2008). Ahtsham Ali, the Prison Service's Muslim adviser, said a 'legitimate Islamic position' meant that Muslims should not discuss their crimes with others, and he was going to hold discussions with officials from the Ministry of Justice: 'I will be taking it forward as a matter of some urgency with colleagues, including those with policy responsibility for the sex offender treatment programme, who are very willing to discuss these issues.' A Prison Service spokeswoman said: 'We are seeking to ensure that the policy for the sex offender treatment programme is sensitive to the diversity of religions within the prison context.' Mark Leech, editor of the *Prisons Handbook*, spoilt the symmetry of this ludicrous liberalism by rather sourly saying that Muslims then risked spending longer in prison because their risk of reoffending could not be assessed.

In May 2008, a review of conditions at maximum-security Whitemoor jail in Cambridgeshire, where 112 of the 400 prisoners are Muslim, said that Muslim prisoners were taking control of the wings. There was, the review said, a reluctance by staff to challenge inappropriate behaviour, 'particularly among black prisoners', and power was shifting from officers to prisoners:

> There was an ongoing theme of fear and instability
> reported by staff in various locations around the prison.
> Many staff seemed to feel a serious incident is imminent.
> The general perception appeared to be that this would
> be a result of the high Muslim population on A wing.
>
> *Times*, 26 May 2008

The review reported that some Muslim prisoners felt they were being harassed, being unfairly identified as gang members. A Prison Service spokesman said that 'a programme of work is planned at Whitemoor to increase mutual understanding between staff and prisoners' (*ibid.*).

It seems to me that the police and the Prison Service are quite properly and necessarily punitive institutions, which, within the rules laid down, command and enforce, rather than suggest or cajole. Orders are to be obeyed, not negotiated; and to be obeyed by all equally. At least, this was the case before the Macpherson Report, ACPO, the Met and the MSF persuaded the guardians of these punitive institutions (and the rest of us) that they were riddled with racial and ethnic prejudice, and that those minorities that were the object of this prejudice had to be endowed with a power to negotiate and determine the terms of their engagement – including, perhaps, the right to accept or refuse engagement at all. Any serious investigation of day-to-day official practices in police forces and prisons would surely show how pervasive is the intrusion into their recruitment and day-to-day policies of organisations like the MSF and its multicultural off-shoots. If 'positive discrimination' is legitimate in the advertising, recruitment and promotional practices of a police force or prison staff, how could it help but become legitimate in their relationships with the 'clientele'?

In January 2008, Sir Ian Blair, Sir Ronnie Flanagan (HM chief inspector of constabulary) and Sir Paul Scott (chief constable of the West Midlands) attended the first annual meeting of the National Association of Muslim Police. The same meeting saw the inauguration of the West Midlands branch of the National Association of Muslim Police. In February 2008, a West Midlands police 'neighbourhood team' (under the general command, though not in the actual presence of, Sergeant Muhammad Shaid) prevented two Christian evangelists from distributing leaflets in Alum Rock. A Pc Loi was present, but evangelist Arthur Cunningham said that it was a police community support officer (PCSO) (either PCSO Naguthney or Ali) who spoke to him, saying that Alum Rock was 'a Muslim area and that they were not allowed to spread the Christian message there'. Arthur Cunningham said that the PCSO told him that he and his colleagues were committing 'a hate crime' by suggesting to Muslim youths that they leave Islam, and that they would be taken to the station if they persisted. Cunningham claimed the PCSO said: 'You have been warned. If you come back here and get beaten up, well, you have been warned.' Furthermore, alleged Arthur Cunningham, the PCSO, on hearing their American accents, also gave them the benefit of a tirade against President Bush and American policies in Iraq and Afghanistan. A West Midlands spokesperson refused to apologise, but said that 'the officer' would be given training in understanding hate crime and communication (*Sunday Telegraph*, 1 June 2008).

Policing by consent – the consent that is of the entire community – is being stealthily replaced with policing by permission, and indeed, by permission of one small and not altogether disinterested sub-set of residents. What we end up with is the kind of confused excuse-manufacturing, hands-off quasi-policing illustrated in the case above and in the following case from *The Times* of 17 March 2008:

Congregation in fear after faith-hate attack on Canon

Canon Michael Ainsworth Rector of St George in the East, Shadwell was put in hospital after an attack on him by two or three Asian youths. His wife said 'Clearly, the Muslim community is very shocked. These individuals were under the influence. And this was a random act, but it may well be that some good can come out of it.'

Allan Ramanoop, an Asian member of the parochial church council, said that parishioners were often scared to challenge the gangs. 'I've been physically threatened and verbally abused on the steps of the church. On one occasion youths shouted: "This should not be a church, this should be a mosque, you should not be here." I just walked away from it – you are too frightened to challenge them... These youths are antichristian.'

Nick Tolson, a former police officer who set up the National Churchwatch safety scheme, said that there had been an increase in faith hate attacks on clergy.

'The harassment is usually coming from young Asian men – often, but not exclusively, Muslim,' he said. 'The police and prosecutors will classify an attack on a mosque or Muslim as a hate crime but not if it is a church or a vicar. These aren't targeted attacks, they are spontaneous, but [the victims] are being singled out because of their faith...'

Rev. Ainsworth later told the *Church Times* (21 March 2008) that his attackers 'swore repeatedly and called me a "fucking priest"', but it was the police who logged the incident as one of 'faith hate'. He pointed out that 'white youths commit similar crimes against churches', and as for his recent attackers 'only if they are caught and tried, on the basis of the evidence which the police have gathered, will we know whether they are Muslims in any real sense of the term. It is important that church-based attacks are treated with the same seriousness as those against mosques and synagogues and other places of worship.' Muslim leaders condemned the attack.

One can only commend Canon and Mrs Ainsworth for their impeccably Anglican response to this outrage: some things remain constant. Other than that, the events at Shadwell, and the reported attitudes of the police and their colleagues, reveal a corroded and degraded system of what can only (though with exaggeration) be called 'social control':

what exactly is an attack that is not 'targeted' but is 'spontaneous', yet also 'singles out' someone on the basis of their religion?

Many years ago, the first joint commissioner of the Metropolitan Police, Richard Mayne (later Sir Richard), told his officers that they were

> To seek and preserve public favour, not by pandering[1] to public opinion; but by constantly demonstrating absolutely impartial service to the law, in complete independence of policy, and without regard to the justice or the injustice of the substance of individual laws, by ready offering of individual service and friendship to all members of the public without regard to their wealth or social standing, by ready exercise of courtesy and friendly good humour; and by ready offering of individual sacrifice in protecting and preserving life.
>
> Dennis, 2005: 80

Ah well.

TERROR

> Ed Husain, a British campaigner against extremism and former radical...urged the Arab street to rise up against the *'default, violent culture'* prevalent in many muslim communities.
>
> Qatar Foundation *Awraq* website,
> Doha Debates, Issue 12 (my italics)

Every restricted society, when it is small and closely unified, alienates itself from the greater whole. Every patriot is severe with strangers: they are merely men,

---

1   In his book, Norman Dennis uses the word 'catering' rather than 'pandering', but in a personal communication tells me that Sir Richard used the word 'pandering' – which seems most apt here.

they are nothing in his eyes. Abroad, the Spartan was ambitious, avaricious, unjust: but disinterestedness, equity and peace reigned within his own walls. Beware of those bookish cosmopolitans who go on distant bookish quests for the duties which they disdain to fulfil in their own surroundings.

Rousseau, *Emile*, in Hampson, 1990: 246

Terror is not simply an expression of multiculturalism, although many of its practitioners have sheltered in that pleasant little hollow. Sikhs have a long-standing military tradition, generally (since the Anglo-Sikh wars) expressed in loyal service to the British Crown. Hindus, too, have a bellicose tradition, carried on in the *kshatriya* (warrior) caste, expressed historically in a series of wars against the encroaching Mughal empire and contemporarily in the *Rashtriya Swayamsevak Sangh*, shock-troops of Hindutva. Yet we, in Britain, have no difficulty with Sikhs and Hindus. No one could now deny that Muslims are deeply involved in violence in and against British society.

The violence we experience at the hands of Muslims is the violence of their civil society, not of the State. We have been formally at war with no Muslim state since the Ottoman Empire declared war and *jihad* on us in 1914/15. At the moment, no Muslim state would appear to be able to engage in military conflict with the West and have even an outside chance of winning – though a nuclear-armed major Muslim state with a well-trained army could probably inflict some kind of defeat on our tiny (British) armed forces. Our armed forces are, of course, unlike those of Bangladesh or Pakistan, since they are either deployed abroad or are at home in barracks. Few of us expect an outbreak of terrorism from British Sikhs or British Hindus, still less from Poles, Australians, Slovakians or Canadians. We do expect it from Muslims resident in Great Britain. Prime Minister Gordon Brown managed to get through his 19 March 2008 statement on the National Security Strategy without mentioning this. He was able, though, to inform the House of Commons that:

to meet the threats ahead, after a trebling of its budget since 2001, the security service will rise in number to 4000, twice the level of 2001... [W]e will be increasing yet again, this time by 10 per cent, the resources for the Joint Terrorism Analysis Centre – which brings together 16 departments including the police and intelligence agencies – and giving it a new focus on the longer-term challenge of investigating the path to violent terrorism... [W]e have set aside funds to modernise our interception capability;...at GCHQ and in the secret intelligence service we are developing new technical capabilities to root out terrorism; and...the new Centre for the Protection of National Infrastructure...will provide a higher level of protection against internet or cyber-based threats.

Gordon Brown, 19 March 2008

Mr Brown had, earlier in his speech, mentioned a plan to 'win over hearts and minds...partnerships for progress and tolerance, involving government, the private and voluntary sectors, community and faith organisations, and individuals'. He went on to talk about a new National Security Forum, involving business, academics, community organisations and security experts from outside government, and he concluded by describing

a new form of civil protection that combines expert preparedness for potential emergencies with greater local engagement of individuals and families themselves. And the Home Secretary and the Communities Secretary will report next month on additional measures we propose for young people, in colleges and universities, and in prisons, and working with faith communities, to disrupt the promoters of violent extremism – all building upon the support of the vast majority of people, of all faiths and backgrounds, who condemn terrorists and their actions.

In December 2007, Home Secretary Jacqui Smith said that the number of terrorists being tracked by the security services had risen from 1,600 to 2,000 *in one year*. In referring to an attempted sale of dirty uranium in Slovakia, she said: 'I think a serious level of threat will be with us over a period of time' (*Daily Telegraph*, 1 December 2007). The government's National Security Strategy of 2008 states that, at any one time, the police and the security and intelligence agencies are contending with around 30 plots, 200 groups or networks and 2,000 individuals (Cabinet Office, 2008). The Royal United Services Institute for Defence and Security Studies (RUSI website, 15 May 2008) commented that a 2005 Home Office and Foreign Office figure of 1 per cent for the number of British Muslims actively engaged in terrorist activity gave something in the region of 16,000 identified terrorists – and this was before the increase in 2008. In 2008, the commissioner of the Metropolitan Police, Sir Ian Blair, told a parliamentary committee that 15 planned terrorist attacks had been foiled since the London bombings of 2005 (*London Evening Standard*, 22 April 2008).

In a way (but only in a way), these relatively small numbers are not the issue. How are these men regarded by their 'communities'? Are they typical of their communities, or atypical but tacitly supported by them, or reluctantly supported by them? Or do these men simply terrorise their communities into at least condoning what they do (or plan to do) by forcing them to look the other way? On the other front, as it were, do the ordinary Muslims in their moderate communities share the view of the *Muslim Directory*, seeing themselves surrounded by the hostile and untrustworthy agencies of the state and by an indifferent or resentful majority society? If so, do they then see in their aggressive co-religionists the defenders, and not the enemies, of their communities, no matter how they might privately deplore the results of actual, real violence and blood on the streets?

Poll after poll shows that a significant minority, usually about 10 per cent of Muslims (or 200,000), support suicide murdering and/or sympathise with militants engaged in such activity. Most of these supporters are young Muslim men. If, to err on the side of caution, we halve this figure and add to it the security service's current estimates (of 2,000 individuals, 200 networks and 30 plots known to them), then we have a small group of deadly serious and very nasty people (mostly young men) floating around in a sea of 100,000 probable sympathisers. Rod Liddle (*Sunday Times*, 5 August 2007) draws our attention to the views of a certain Haras Rafiq, a government adviser. Mr Rafiq told the Channel 4 *Dispatches* programme that one British Muslim in eleven – almost 10 per cent – backed terrorist bomb attacks, and that a further 20 per cent 'sympathised' with those who carry out such attacks. Liddle comments that this is something like '400,000-plus British citizens ready to either strap on the Semtex or smile indulgently while someone else does so'. Every fifth Muslim you meet falls within Mr Liddle's description. If you halve the figures of Rafiq and Liddle, then every tenth Muslim you meet on the street harbours or condones serious hostility towards you. Furthermore, comments Liddle, a poll last year had 40 per cent of British Muslims wanting *shariah* law imposed on Britain. The percentage of those who support or 'empathise' with terrorist attacks increases when Israelis and Jews are the chosen victims.

It is almost inconceivable that the security services and the police know all that there is. In May 2008, explosions in Exeter prompted a security service review of intelligence: 'Our map was pretty near empty over the West Country. Now we're tempted to put a big warning sign over the whole area' (*Daily Telegraph*, 26 May 2008). The *Daily Telegraph* listed over 224 terrorist 'hot spots' of groups in the United Kingdom. Various 'reformed jihadists' such as Hassan Butt and Ed Husain speak quite openly about 'networks' of 'hardened radicals' (Hassan Butt, *Sunday Times*, 20 April 2008); while in *The Islamist*, Ed Husain states that 'every single Muslim group in Britain' was discussing (and was unable to refute) his and Hizb-ut-Tahrir's ideas on the existence of a state of war with the West and the propriety of 'lying and deception' in order to win this war (Husain, 2007: 100–01).

The newly moderate Husain wants Hizb to be banned; but Yahya Birt points out that Hizb has about 8,500 members and that the 'ripple effect' of banning it would be 'immense...and the other effect would be the chilling of the dissident political voice of young Muslims who would no doubt draw their own conclusions' (Birt, 2008). One wonders whether these young men do actually gather 'in groups', and, if so, how many of these groups there are, how many people there are in them, and how many (if any) felt any obligation whatsoever to inform the police of what was going on. In trial after terrorist trial, no one (everyone protests), but no one, knew what that nice young man next door was planning to do. And if they did know, what should they do? On 11 May 2008, the *Sunday Telegraph* reported that Hassan Butt, the ex-extremist who claimed to have been a recruiter for al-Qaeda, had been arrested. Would this arrest encourage or discourage Mr Butt's successors to come clean and tell the police what they had been up to? Yahya Birt's website review of *The Islamist* elicited a long discussion of what to do about Hizb-ut-Tahrir – to ban or not to ban. Just as interesting was the discussion about Ed Husain, there being a clear view that he had been suborned by the British security services and that he was, in fact, a traitor (see below).

This grievance–defensive–aggression mechanism derives, as far as one can see, from the belief, widespread in the Muslim *ummah*, that everyone but Muslims is involved in terrorism: in the *Daily Telegraph* of 12 January 2008, Damian Thompson commented that, in Indonesia, Egypt, Turkey, Jordan and Pakistan, a Pew poll showed a majority of people saying that Arabs were not responsible for the 9/11 attacks; that 56 per cent of Muslims resident in Britain thought that Arabs were innocent of those attacks; and that 25 per cent of Muslims resident in Great Britain thought that the British government was 'in some way' involved in the 7 July 2005 bombings in London. So 500,000 Muslims resident in the United Kingdom believe that HM Government in some way assisted several Muslim men in tying on vests of explosives and in exploding those vests, themselves and many other (innocent) people on the London Underground? Where on earth do these ideas come from?

In 2005, Anthony Glees and Chris Pope published an account of the terrorist and/or extremist presence and activity at British universities. Of the 31 universities for which they had information, 20 (60 per cent) had Islamist groups, another four had both British National Party (BNP) and Islamist groups, and six had a BNP group only. One university – Oxford – boasted a violent animal rights group (Glees and Pope, 2005). Glees and Pope's account was followed by the Department for Innovation, Universities and Skills (DIUS) publication *Promoting Good Campus Relations, Fostering Shared Values and Preventing Violent Extremism in Universities and Higher Education Colleges*. This identified 'Al-Qa'ida influenced terrorism' as the main threat, and analysed the way in which, in higher education, young people could easily be 'groomed' by terrorists: 'Universities and colleges can provide a recruiting ground for extremists of all forms, particularly those that target young people.' In 2007, Denis MacEoin published, for Policy Exchange, *The Hijacking of British Islam: How Extremist Literature is Subverting Mosques in the UK* (MacEoin, 2007). A highly irresponsible BBC *Newsnight* programme sought, on the basis of minor and very 'curious' errors, to rubbish this report. Yet this in no way diminishes the seriousness of its basic findings – that extremist and violently anti-Western literature is available at Muslim bookshops and mosques throughout the UK, and that this literature is being published, distributed, bought – and presumably read – by Muslim networks and Muslim citizens of the UK. In 2007/08, too, three Channel 4 *Dispatches* programmes provided evidence of (to put it mildly) a wide hostility to the 'host society' on the part of many Muslims.

In 2007, Policy Exchange published *Living Apart Together. British Muslims and the Paradox of Multiculturalism*, by Munira Mirza and others, which analyses the large and growing divisions between this 'host society' and the Muslims who have chosen to live in it (Mirza, 2007). In 2008, the Institute of Community Cohesion (iCoCo), a government-sponsored academic unit, published *Understanding and Appreciating Muslim Diversity: Towards Better Engagement and Participation* (a cheerful little title!), which told us that 'Muslim communities are "withdrawing" into ethno-national and theologically based groupings in response to the prolonged focus on extremism at national level. This has the effect of increasing inter-community tensions' (iCoCo, 2008: 4). Also in 2008, the Centre for Social Cohesion published *Crimes of the Community: Honour-Based Violence in the UK*, by James Brandon and Salam Hafez. This told us, among other things, that about 65,000 women in the UK have undergone some form of genital mutilation; and that – far from such practices dying out – younger British-born Muslims are adopting these and other methods of 'reinforcing traditional codes of behaviour' (Brandon and Hafez, 2008: 78). In different ways, all these documents paint a picture of a series of discrete Muslim communities folding themselves into self-regarding, self-defensive, quasi-autonomous social entities, amenable as much to siren songs of enmity as to the blandishments of Western ideas – let alone the amiable buffooneries of the British government. The weight of the evidence indicates that things are getting worse, not better.

Moderate Britons (like me) could perhaps be forgiven for thinking that the 2,000 MI5-identified terrorists swim in a very large and supportive sea.

In that sea will be large numbers of fellow-travelling fish and larger numbers of frightened fish. Violence, as my friends from Ireland told me, is as much directed in as out: violent men will not scruple in maintaining their anonymity and implementing their plans by, if necessary, threatening those who might be tempted to try to stop them or to inform on them. In self-contained 'communities' such as those in which most Muslims live, the mechanisms of social control, including violence, will tend to give a high level of licence to young and violent men. The terror can be quite remote: an anticipated perhaps-possibility as much as a here-and-now reality. I offer a rather ordinary example. A couple of years ago, an Iraqi acquaintance of mine came back from the university mosque and handed me, with almost no comment, some 'Islamist' literature. I didn't really know what it was, and he was somewhat diffident about telling me. Anyway, what was I to do with it? Had I gone to the police, they would have wanted to know where it came from and who had given it to me; they might have wanted to run it past their Muslim 'community' advisers (had they any); and they might knock on my door, as well as on my acquaintance's door. What trouble would he, his wife and his children have been in if I had set the police on his trail? Should I perhaps instead have gone to the university vice-chancellor? To what level of an uninterested or even hostile university bureaucracy might I have been referred, and with what result? Would the university really have wanted to know what was (or might be) going on in its 'own' mosque (raising, among other things, the question of why it has a mosque in the first place)? And was it all a fuss about nothing, anyway? I wanted neither the bother nor the risk; so I binned the incriminating document, and the mosque flourishes. Whether it is a hotbed of Islamism, I do not know.

Perhaps things are changing, and perhaps Muslims are themselves finding a way of dealing with the 'default' violence in their midst. In commenting on his involvement with the Quilliam Foundation, ex-Islamist Ed Husain says that: 'For the first time in Western Muslim history a Muslim group is challenging extremists using a scriptural and theological paradigm' (*Sunday Times*, 20 April 2008). Husain's Quilliam Foundation clearly has a lot of ground to make up; and I describe below some of the reaction to him from some of his fellow Muslims. The iCoCo report and reports by Policy Exchange indicate that the enmity and disaffection so deeply rooted in Islam is a growing problem, not a declining one. I have already mentioned the publications that document the widespread availability of extremist literature in Muslim bookshops, and I have referred to Anthony Glees' data about Islamic radicalisation inside mosques attached to British universities. The careers of Hassan Butt and Ed Husain are revealing in many ways – not least in the fact that neither Hassan Butt nor Ed Husain, throughout years of Islamist activity, was ever stopped in his tracks by the security services.

Perhaps things have indeed already changed – but in some quixotic ways. In 2007, Home Secretary Jacqui Smith asked the British public to remain vigilant over the Christmas period, as there was an increased threat of terrorist attacks in public places, including from radioactive dirty bombs (*Daily Telegraph*, 1 December 2007). Ms Smith has noticed that Islam in Britain is becoming embedded in its many and various communities, the 'protests' of its sundry religious 'leaders' now being taken with a large fistful of salt by our now alerted politicians. Hence the peculiar and almost risible spectacle of a British home secretary negotiating with the government of Pakistan for a supply of government-approved and certificated imams! Home Secretary Jacqui Smith struck a deal with Pakistan to import 'moderate Muslim' clerics to combat extremism in British mosques. Said she:

> the vast majority of British Muslims have a Pakistani heritage... We need to do more to tackle those places where radicalisation is developing – in prisons, schools, higher education – so that people are getting the right message about what it means to be a British Muslim. We will also work to ensure we identify vulnerable people being groomed for terror – in the same way we protect young people from being dragged into crime and abuse.
>
> *Daily Telegraph*, 16 April 2008

As I said earlier, Muslims, at about 2 per cent of the general population, now constitute about 9 or 10 per cent of the prison population. These are by no means all terrorists – at least they weren't when they went into prison. A report in the *Daily Telegraph* (15 April 2008) said that prison staff at Belmarsh prison were insufficiently trained to 'fight radicalisation without alienating Muslims'. No more, perhaps, than are academics who, according to Anthony Glees, are liable to find terrorist cells in their educational institutions

(Glees and Pope, 2005). Mr Bill Rammell, minister of state for higher education and lifelong learning at DIUS, lent his name to an official response to Professor Glees' concerns in the document mentioned above (*Promoting Good Campus Relations, Fostering Shared Values and Preventing Violent Extremism in Universities and Higher Education Colleges*), which noted that universities had, in addition to terrorist threats, to deal with animal rights activists, anti-Semitism, Islamophobia, and wider issues of race, faith, sexual orientation and gender intolerance (not to mention teaching, quality assessments and research assessment exercises and getting on with the job). Continuing in this vein, and capping what would, on its own, have been a fair target for satire, Mr Rammell's colleagues in government announced plans to recruit Muslim women in the battle for community cohesion and the war against terror. Shelina Zahra Janmohamed, showing some humour, greeted this with 'Using Muslim Women as Trojan Horses' (an interesting analogy), writing that 'The Government's latest announcement...confuses social cohesion with extremism'. She went on:

> Apparently we're not very assertive. And apparently, we need the Government's help. And apparently, some training courses are going to solve the problem. Thus spoke the Government when announcing that they would help us Muslim women to stop extremism. Once we've been suitably trained, we'll go on to spy on our kids, create community cohesion, and curb terror. We'll then stop for afternoon tea. [Afterwards], we'll reverse global warming and achieve world peace.
> Shelina's blog: Islam Online website, 28 January 2008

In spite of all that, with exaggeration clearly expressing truths that otherwise cannot be voiced, Shelina thought the money being made available was acceptable. Shelina's humorous defensiveness is as revealing as is the reaction of Muslim web-riders to a review of Ed Husain's book, *The Islamist*. Husain, who remains a devout Muslim and is active in what must be regarded as more moderate pursuits such as the Quilliam Foundation, was for five years an Islamic fundamentalist, involved in and familiar with the workings of Muslim terrorist groups operating in London. In May 2008, his book was reviewed by Yahya Birt, a 'revert' (convert) to Islam, and the web manager of 'Musings on the Britannic Crescent'. Birt's review of Husain's book generated 22 responses, one of which was from Husain himself. All the correspondents were (going by their names) Muslims, and most were men. What struck me was the general note of censure visited *upon Husain* for opening up Islam to 'public' – i.e. non-Muslim – comment and criticism. His motives were impugned – 'this is a book written with a distinct motive and an agenda...a tell-all book, attacking all and sundry' – and when Husain himself entered the site, he was asked: 'Are you a government agent?' 'Why do Melanie Philips, David Aaronovitch and Michael Gove support your work – doesn't that give rise to suspicion about your work?' 'If you're not a government agent, do you work for the secret services?' 'Why do you name and shame prominent Muslims and national Muslim organisations in your book?' 'Don't you realise the British are using you?'

References were made to Husain's alleged support for the *kufr* or *kafir* government of Syria, the criticism being of the Ba'athist Syrian government, which massacred thousands of Muslim Brotherhood members in the city of Hama. But perhaps of greater significance is the use of the word *kufr* or *kafir*, the all-purpose derogatory and insulting term for all non-Muslims. It is difficult to believe that such a term would have been used in this intra-Muslim conversation, had a *kafir* like me been expected to log onto the website.

On 22 February 2008, the *Muslim Weekly* 'Feature' column dealt with 'Brotherhood in Islam'. 'Islam', says the writer, 'has taken every necessary measure to preserve humanity from division and discord.' Among these arrangements is:

> Concealing the fault of others: A believer must conceal the faults of his brother, no matter how great those

faults might be, so long as his brother is not open about them. He must do so to protect the dignity of his brother and to protect him from falling into public disgrace... The bond of brotherhood is different than other bonds that exist between people. It has a far deeper effect on the nature of society than any other bond, like that of language, national identity, or common interests.

Shelina clearly is not going to 'spy' on her children, and Mr Husain's interlocutors clearly assume that 'spying' involves opening up the internal machinations of the brotherhood of the Muslim world to 'the British', *kafirs* like me. Such 'defensiveness', configured in that way – Muslims versus *kafirs* – is precisely what makes Muslim terrorism so 'safe' for its practitioners. And what, to repeat (because it is so revealing), are we, the moderate people of Great Britain, to make of that outburst by Muhammad Abdul Bari, secretary-general of the MCB, when he threatened us with 'two million Muslim terrorists – 700,000 of them in London'? Mr Bari would appear to have found a degree of plasticity in the Muslim community, well beyond the wildest accusations of the BNP. Prisons, schools, universities, mosques, bookshops – too many of them, at one time or another, shown to be repositories of, and safe havens for, murderous ideas and intentions. Where does it all stop?

Well, the eminent and moderate Tim Winter (aka Abdal Hakim Murad) offers the following, already quoted:

> The current wave of zealotry will, I have no doubt, pass away as rapidly as it came, perhaps after some climacteric Masada. Some souls will have been damaged by it, and the historians will note, with a regretful curiosity, how Islam was, for a few years, associated with terrorism. But the extremism will disappear, because no one who has a future really desires it.
>
> Seddon *et al.*, 2003: 21

In its way, this is as extraordinary a remark as the one produced by Muhammad Abdul Bari: what, even by analogy, has Masada to do with Muslims living here? Are the murderous suicide bombers who killed civilians on London trains to be compared to Eleazar ben Yair and the Jews who, after genuinely heroic resistance to the occupying armies of Rome, killed themselves rather than submit to alien control and contempt? Given the threatening smug stupidity of such remarks, it is hardly a criticism of the perceptiveness of the British population at large that 60 per cent of a representative sample of them believed that racial tensions were likely to spill over into more violence (*Daily Telegraph*, 18 April 2008).

Considering the terrorist networks' ability to rebuild and to find new havens, the influence of radical doctrines on the young of many countries, the difficulty of encouraging economic and political reform in the Arab and Muslim world, the demographic explosion of developing countries, the very modest performance of those countries in areas of education and employment, and our own inadequacies in the West, there is every reason to think that terrorism is indeed a long-term threat.

Delpech, 2007: 87

CHAPTER 6

RELIGION: THEIRS, OURS

WOMAN JAILED FOR 'WORSHIPPING TEA POT'

A Sharia court in Malaysia jailed a woman for two years for joining a 'tea-pot worshipping cult'.

Kamariah Ali, a 57 year old former teacher, was arrested in 2005 when the government...demolished the two storey high sacred tea pot and other infrastructure of the 'heretical' Sky Kingdom cult...

[I]n Malaysia, despite constitutional guarantees of freedom of worship, born Muslims such as Mrs Ali are forbidden from converting to other religions. Passing sentence, the Sharia judge Mohammed Abdullah said: 'The court is not convinced that the accused has repented and is willing to abandon any teachings contrary to Islam. I pray God will open the doors of your heart, Kamariah.'

Mrs Ali has already been jailed once for apostasy, for 20 months in 1992. 'This has to stop. They can't be sending her again and again to prison for this,' her lawyer, Sa'adiah Din, told reporters.

'She informed the court that she is not a Muslim.'
Daily Telegraph online, 16 March 2008

A Church, then, I take to be a voluntary society of men, joining themselves together of their own accord, in order for the public worshipping of God, in such a manner as they judge acceptable to him, and effectual to the salvation of their souls. I say it is a free and voluntary society. Nobody is born a member of any Church; otherwise the religion of the parents would descend upon the children, by the same right of inheritance as their temporal estates, and everyone would hold his faith by the same tenure as he holds his lands; than which nothing can be imagined more absurd...

No man by nature is bound under any particular Church or sect, but everyone joins himself voluntarily to that society in which he believes he has found that profession and worship which is truly acceptable to God... if afterwards he discovers anything erroneous... why should it not be as free for him to go out as to enter?

John Locke, in Grayling, 2007: 74, 304

The kettle o' the Kirk and State,
Perhaps a clout may fall in't;
But deil a foreign tinkler loun
Shall ever ca' a nail in't.
Our fathers' blude the kettle bought,
And wha wad dare to spoil it,
By Heav'ns! The sacrilegious dog
Shall fuel be to boil it!
By Heav'ns! The sacrilegious dog
Shall fuel be to boil it!

Robert Burns, 'Does Haughty Gaul
Invasion Threat?', 1795

As I said before, I have, even in a chapter entitled 'Religion', absolutely no intention of getting involved in theological disputes. While I will no doubt find it impossible to avoid occasional reference to the Bible or to the Qur'an, I am basically concerned with the role played by religious cultures and institutions in our society – the historical and the socio-cultural, not the theological. I should say that I am a communicant pew-occupying grumbling member of the Church of England, whose consistent idiocies are its greatest commendation.

For better or for worse, we natives have taken away from religion and from religious leaders and their theological pronouncements whatever public or political authority they might once have had. Nothing is so serious as to put it beyond satire – until the BBC came along and conferred this immunity upon Islam, thereby perhaps consoling Muslims but certainly affronting me and my friends. The insistence by the director-general of the BBC, speaking at Westminster Cathedral (Islamist Watch website, 15 April 2008), that Islam was treated like any other religion does not now console: the very fact that such a thing has to be said shows how corrupted we and the BBC have become. In the way of our tolerant (and frightened) liberalism, a 'minority privilege' has been conferred upon this one religion, thereby encouraging it in its exclusivism and in the angry 'defence' of its innumerable sensitivities.

Difficulty arises when Moderate Muslims and we moderate natives come to discuss religion. It is, of course, immediately obvious that 'Muslim' denotes a basis for defining and proclaiming identity that is now almost unknown in Western Europe. I know very few British people who regard their religious beliefs as the mark of their primary identity. Given that (and other things), the Moderate Muslim may well think that even his church-going acquaintance is essentially *irreligious* because he neither shares nor practises nor appreciates the Muslim version of religion. This sense may well lead the Muslim observer to see little difference between moderate Christian natives (like me) and moderate convinced atheists (like my eldest son). It is necessary to advise such an observer to beware of too ready a subscription to the idea that the great masses of us moderate British people are somehow 'opposed to religion' (some are), or irreligious, or hostile to, or bigoted and stupid about such things. Shabash Batta makes that mistake when, responding to an editorial question 'Should Jesus remain at the heart of Christmas?', he writes that:

> The problem with modern Britain is that the whites are losing their culture – which is why they feel so threatened by Islam. If the indigenous Brits retained more of their religious identity, then they would understand other people's more.
>
> *Eastern Eye – the Voice of British Asians*,
> 21 December 2007

It takes some effort to swallow the extraordinary cheek implicit in the original editorial question – can you imagine the offence in the Muslim world if the *Daily Telegraph* or the *Evening Standard* were to ask: 'Should Muhammad be at the heart of the *hijrah*, or the *kabah* at the heart of the *haj*?' Christians do their religion differently, Mr Batta. But even the most liberal and moderate of us would find it difficult to comprehend Christmas without Christ.

Earlier on, I said that I was going to avoid the delights of theological and exegetical discourse, and proceed on the basis that Islam is what Muslims do (just as, of course, Christianity is what Christians do). Muslims, moderate or otherwise, are much more likely to be routinely religious and religiously active than are their moderate British friends and neighbours: figures on daily prayer and mosque attendance indicate a very much higher level for the Muslim version of religion (see, for example, the Lausanne World Pulse website, March 2007). I am aware that Muslims, like others who attend religious services, may be there more in body than in spirit. It is obviously the case that Islam, like Christianity, has room for constructive hypocrisy. I grew up in a Muslim town, Mombasa, and it was a Muslim friend from there who introduced me to alcohol. In reply to my comment that I thought Islam forbade alcohol, he replied: 'Sure, and Christianity forbids adultery.' Fair point. Not all Muslims are 'devout', any more than are all Christians or Hindus. Like

Hindu men (see below, Chapter 7), Muslim men seem to have an interest in such irreligious things as pornography (Abdullah, 2007).

However, various surveys show that about half of all Muslims attend one or other of the major annual festivals (the comparative figure for Christians is less than half that); weekly mosque attendance is also about twice that of Christians. Endless surveys document the decline of British Christianity, from 55 per cent church attendance in 1851 (the famous 'religious census') to about 6 per cent today. Policy Exchange's 2007 report *Living Apart Together* (Mirza, 2007: 5) shows that 71 per cent of Muslims resident in Britain pray daily (49 per cent five times a day; 22 per cent between one and three times a day). I would be astounded if 1 per cent of the small number of self-defined Christians prayed more than five times a week! Muslim women are more devout than are Muslim men. For 86 per cent of Muslims, religion is the most important thing in their lives (the same being true for 11 per cent of the general British population). Of young Muslims under 34, 41 per cent said they defined themselves first and foremost as Muslims (the figure for older Muslims (over 35) is 30 per cent). Thus, contrary to what is going on in Christianity, young Muslims seem more, not less, likely than their parents to find their character in Muslim practice. Such data further reinforce one of my main points: that the Muslims in Britain are currently engaged in the elaboration of an increasingly defensive and exclusive community, with its boundaries stalwartly defined and protected, especially by the young.

In 2002, the *Guardian* series on 'Muslim Britain' provided a picture of Highfields, an inner-city area of Leicester. 'The old churches scattered across Highfields', wrote Gerard Seenan,

> do not have much of a congregation these days. The number of Christians who call that part of inner-city Leicester home has dwindled to almost nothing. On a Friday afternoon not even a vicar can be glimpsed

among their pews. At the mosques, though, it is a different story.

Elderly bearded men dressed in flowing whites and creams are helped through the doors by grandsons dressed in baggy jeans and flashy trainers. Local businessmen mix with mechanics in their Friday best. On the streets outside almost every woman wears a hijab; many are clothed in burkas, only their eyes are exposed to the rare midday sun...

From the minute you walk into Highfields, it's impossible not to notice that Islam is the thread which binds the community together. 'Our religion, our culture and our community are inseparable,' says Yaqub Khan, a local community leader. Outward signs are obvious: the shops sell halal food; there are mosques on every second street corner...

It is [now] the young who fill Leicester's mosques. Those who were without direction a few years ago have grown up and, largely, turned to Islam – not just as a religion, but as a full cultural identity. In the evening their children attend the madrassahs; in the daytime, if they can find places, they go to the local, private Islamic schools...

Guardian, 20 June 2002

Seenan quotes the chairman of the Federation of Muslim Organisations in Leicester as saying that 'Ordinary Muslims tend to turn to the mosque or community leaders' rather than to local politicians, who are 'not much involved in the community; they tend to toe the party line more often than the community line'...

In the afternoon the congregation at the community centre's mosque sits rapt. The imam, like most of his colleagues, comes from Pakistan and gives a traditional sermon in Urdu: eternal damnation for those who live an immoral life, paradise for those who behave well.

ibid.

Islam, as practised in close (or closed?) British communities like Highfields, provides a form of religion and religious life that is rather alien even to the relatively few of us British who are religious. It is almost impossible for Christians to actually live in Britain surrounded by a Christian community. Such things no longer exist. When my wife and I walk to church on Sunday, we walk through streets and past houses on which the very existence of a church has little apparent effect. The Easter Procession around the church grounds is carried on in front of passers-by and observers to whom we and our banners and our singing may as well come from Papua New Guinea for all the comprehension they have of it.

In the *Muslim Weekly*, Maryam Dadabhoy, in introducing us to the Arabic term *Zikr*, 'the remembrance of Allah', provides us with another interesting contrast between Muslim and Western or European religion. While Ms Dadabhoy, it has to be said, seems to me to be somewhat immoderately dismissive of our own native religious practices, she is correct in telling us that '*Zikr* Sets Muslims Apart From People of Other Faiths'. *Zikr*, she tells us, is the Arabic term for the remembrance of Allah, denoting the 'complete way of life' that is Islam:

No other religion perfectly incorporates every-minute aspects into life. Muslims start any and everything that they do with the words 'Audhubillahi Minashaytaanirajeem, Bismillah ir Rahman ir Rahim' (I seek refuge in Allah from the accursed devil, in the Name of Allah, the most Gracious, the most Merciful).

Islam teaches us how to greet people, how to eat, how to sleep, how to leave one's home, how to dress, how to behave, even how to cut our nails...

The greatest form of *Zikr* though is the fear of Allah. A Hadith of the holy Prophet Muhammad (pbuh) states that a Muslim should think of death forty times everyday... Anyone who worships Allah at the prescribed times and remembers Allah before going to sleep, then the entire time he is sleeping he is performing

Zikr...because he is sleeping with Allah's permission...
    As it is obvious, Islam is not just a religion, but a complete way of life.

Muslim Weekly, 29 February 2008

'Religion, for followers of other faiths,' she explains,

consists of once a week attendance at temples and churches and the wearing of a religious symbol around their necks. Religion has the last priority in most people's lives. They are too busy partying, making money and having too much fun to stop and think about where their lives are going. It is no surprise that so many people revert to Islam, both non-Muslims and born Muslims. Most reverts claim they felt emptiness while worshipping in their old faiths. Islam replaced that void in their lives, Alhamdu Lillah (thanks be to Allah).

ibid.

British people, for sure, do not share the *Zikr* version of religion. This is true even of that small percentage of British people who, like me, are practising Christians, the 10 per cent of British people who join me in regular church attendance – and the number is declining. We do our religion differently. Apart from putting in highly irregular church appearances, most British are happy to shop, drink, play and socialise on a Sunday, which has pretty well lost its special status. Only at the time of death is some form of religious phrasing spoken over the departed soul and his kith and kin. I use the term 'religious phrasing' because by no stretch of the imagination could the average crematorium performance be deemed a service, a liturgy: I have presided over such a 'phrasing' myself. Funeral services at crematoria are notable for the almost total lack of experience and competence at hymn singing and liturgical niceties on the part of the assembled mourners.

Young Muslims growing up in the West are denied the constant reminders of their Creator that are observed in

Muslim countries. It is difficult for them to believe that 'God Willing' used to preface people's actions in Britain before the country was secularized, just as '*Insha Allah*', with exactly the same meaning, is used by Muslims today.

Azami, 2004: 5

While we may agree with Mr Azami that Britain is 'secularised', it would not be wise for him or anyone else to assume that most British people are convinced atheists. About 8 per cent of British people so define themselves, while another 10 per cent regard themselves as agnostic. (Such people are, of course, a presence – and an indigenous presence – in the UK in numbers that are considerably in excess of the *combined* total of Muslims, Hindus, Sikhs, Jews, etc.) In the 2001 census, 72 per cent of the British defined themselves as 'Christian', though, as already noted, less than 10 per cent of the British are regular churchgoers (though another 20–30 per cent pay a visit at least once a year). The rest (60 per cent) do not enter a church from one year to the next. The Anglican Church, in particular, is difficult to understand. Some years ago, an Anglican minister announced from the pulpit that he no longer believed in God – and then, when he was in consequence sacked, sued his employer for unfair dismissal! Idiosyncratic, perhaps: but there is something about British Christianity and British religious practice that confers upon its moderate practitioners a stance seemingly very different from that of Moderate Muslims. In 2008, the bishop of Rochester, in urging the conversion of Muslims, found himself criticised for suggesting such a thing by a fellow Anglican bishop, the Rt. Rev Stephen Lowe, bishop of urban life and faith. Bishop Lowe said that the bishop of Rochester 'shows no sensitivity to the need for good interfaith relations', adding that 'Christians, Jews, Muslims, Hindus and Sikhs are learning to respect one another's paths to God'. The bishop of Rochester said that, while it was quite right to be sensitive to Muslims, we were 'a nation rooted in the Christian faith', and that, while he welcomed people of other faiths, 'you cannot have an honest conversation on the basis of a fudge' (*Daily Telegraph*, 26 May 2008). The contending forces will battle it out at General Synod, Fudgeguns at 20 paces.

Paradoxically, perhaps, the nature and actual strength of British religion can be measured best by emphasising the extent to which it shares in the institutional arrangements and culture of British secularism and humanism, rather than by the actual numbers of worshippers and churchgoers. How else to explain, for example, the taken-for-grantedness of *Desert Island Discs*, when, before offering the castaway a choice of luxuries, the host assures him or her that he or she 'already has the Bible and Shakespeare'? These apparently opposed writings, representing quite different systems of thought, in fact share a common meta-narrative – not least their fundamental Englishness, itself an idiosyncratic player in the history of the Christian West. Engels, looking forward to the triumph of English secularism, rather whimsically noted years ago that 'agnosticism though not yet considered the thing quite as much as the Church of England, is yet nearly on a par as far as respectability goes with Baptism and decidedly ranks above the Salvation Army' (MacIntyre, 1967: 9). Engels expected the popular challenger 'agnosticism' to replace the ranks of Anglicans, Baptists and Salvationists as the champion of English 'respectability'. Engels was, of course, wrong – at least in the short to medium term; he might soon enough be right. In particular, Engels was unaware that the apparently Erastian nature of what appears to be, in England, an 'established' Church, obscures the very real triumph of the 'Enlightenment' project or 'agnosticism' in helping, to use Brian Barry's term, to 'privatise' or 'civilise' religion(s) – and thus to prolong and fructify their lives. By 'civilise' or 'privatise', I mean that religious institutions simply take their place in the unruly scrum of civil society, accepting (more or less) society's liberal ground rules, and making no claim for extensive or exclusive privilege within the constitutional law-making system of the state. It is well within the sense of this general liberal precept that religious practices, rooted in a *national tradition*, should be respected, in that changes in them should be broadly acceptable and not undertaken at the insistence of, or in the interests of, particular groups. Privatised religion can operate only within a long-established and slowly evolving national culture; such religion does not have to be the 'glue' of the state, because the glue comes from a secular source. It is perhaps unnecessary to repeat, with John Locke, that no religion so conceived should assume that it can, so to speak, 'inherit' its members, seeing and treating them as fixed recruits, generation upon generation. A privatised religion assumes the propriety, and indeed the necessity, of free individualism, in religious life as in political life.

Ever since the Civil War, there has been a plurality of Christianities in Britain – indeed, in a limited sense, a variety of faiths, Jews being invited back by Cromwell after an absence of nearly 400 years. The eventual 'winners' of the English Civil War, the American Colonists (many of whom returned to England to fight for Parliament in the war), were clear indeed that the state should 'make no law in respect of religion', and in the United States created *de novo* (but not *ex nihilo*) a liberal and religiously plural society, which has in its basics never changed. It is perhaps precisely because it was 'privatised' that American Christianity has flourished. In England, the Declaration of Indulgence of the restored Charles II may have turned out to have been longer in the ignoring than in the drafting; but even through the years of the Test Acts and the Acts of Uniformity, variants of Christianity other than Anglicanism lived quietly and grew steadily, led as much by theology as by embedded ascription to Colonel Rainsborough's insistence that 'the poorest he that is in England has a life to live, as the greatest he'. Henry Ireton's retort, that political influence should be restricted to those who had a 'permanent fixed interest in this kingdom', is also part of our religious and civil inheritance. The Putney Debates of 1647, at which Rainsborough and Ireton spoke, laid out, for *pro tem* losers and *pro tem* winners, the basis on which British civil society and British religious life would develop throughout the 18th and 19th centuries. (The debates should, incidentally, be required reading for all who would settle here.) In 1861, Robert Hall, a great Baptist preacher, summed up the sense of history of English religious life:

> From the time of Elizabeth, under whom they [the Dissenters] began to make their appearance, their views of religious liberty have gradually extended... Having thus been directed by a train of events into the right path, they pushed their principles to their legitimate consequences, and began to discern the impropriety of all religious establishments whatsoever.
>
> Robert Hall, in Cowherd, 1959: 23

The experience of the First World War in a way reinforced these older ideas of religious 'liberty', and certainly directed Anglican religious thinking in the direction of a kind of active-egalitarian quietism and pacifism. Alan Wilkinson, discussing Scott Holland's thoughts on what the war did to men, writes that: 'The more men were drawn to an alliance with the crucified, the more impossible would it be to express sacrifice in terms of killing' (Wilkinson, 1978: 258). Others expressed this rather more brusquely, Wilkinson telling the story of the clergyman who got into a carriage full of soldiers returning to the front:

> He enthusiastically exclaimed: So, you are going to fight God's war? No response; he repeated his statement. Again silence. Then he asked: Don't you believe this is God's war? Silence, broken after a while by: Sir, hadn't you better keep your poor Friend out of this bloody mess?
>
> *ibid.*: 231

Whether because of the war, or because of the longer developments indicated by Robert Hall, Christianity in England, and indeed in much of Europe, came to prefer a voluntary framework for its religious practice, and, by extension, to withdraw its support for compulsion or punitive methods of societal and governmental construction and management. As the 20th century progressed, these attitudes, this free

English society, this gentled English religion, developed even further. As Brian Barry rather grudgingly puts it:

> If Christianity has in the last fifty years finally become compatible with civility (at least in most of Western Europe), that is the long term consequence of an assault on its pretensions that got under way seriously in the eighteenth century. Gibbon employed the stiletto, while Voltaire resorted to the rapier.
>
> Barry, 2006: 31

Barry is again (somewhat diffidently) drawing our attention to the fact that, for many decades now, the main religion of Europe, Christianity, has become what he calls 'privatised' or 'civilised'. There is no particular reason to accept his argument that this was due exclusively to purely secular writers, no matter how influential they might have been: he appears to be ignorant of the Putney Debates. However, Barry rightly insists that, in a liberal society (and moderate Christians, in a liberal state, and along with liberal atheists, agnostics and deists, tend to be liberal), the state should 'take no interest' in religion, favouring none, and requiring only that the religious institutions of the national society should operate according to liberal principles, broadly accepted. Religions which conform to liberal principles, or which carry them within their historical memory – their 'soul', so to speak – demonstrate an inclination to operate as voluntary institutions with little ambition or need for public or monopolistic power. When they are, to use Barry's terminology, 'privatised', they make no pretence at spreading their control through the institutions of the state; neither does their existence require the suppression of the existence of other religions.

'The position of Islam is rather different', Barry says. 'No polity with a Muslim majority has ever given rise to a stable liberal democratic state.' And he dismisses 'modern forms of politicized Islam as pathological reactions to modernity' (*ibid.*: 27). He refers to Charles Taylor, who also insists that Islam is incompatible with liberalism; and, as unwitting proof of his thesis, he refers to a book by the Muslim scholar Yusuf al-Qaradawi (to whom I have earlier referred). Qaradawi is quoted as insisting that the Qur'an provides the answers to *all* questions of 'administration, property and legitimate politics', and that 'Islam declares openly that it includes all aspects of human life, material and spiritual, individual and social' (*ibid.*: 332). Given that attitude, there seems to be little question of a 'privatising' of Islam. Unlike Muslims, Christians do not have to reach for scriptural 'proof' that 'there is no compulsion in religion': it is unthinkable here. I can think of no one I know who would register anything but total disbelief should a man or a woman be either compelled to believe in this god rather than that god, or punished for dropping this god in favour of that god.

Our daily lives and religious practices are proof of it. There is no compulsion at all in our version of the Christian religion, and no understanding either of why any religion should find recourse to it either necessary or commendable. British Christians, and most definitely the Church of England, are fundamentally (*sic*) opposed to all forms of coercion. Indeed, as the bishop of Rochester found out, few British Christians now wish to see their faith rigorously propagated, never mind monopolistically 'enforced'. *Belief* may well, in the believers, be strong; but *confidence*, arrogance, the compulsion to proselytise, the desire to compel, the zeal to triumph, is weak. This applies, too, to those social and sexual arrangements on which there have been, for centuries, Christian rules and expectations, but which are now seen as matters for socio-political and/or individual decision. There is almost no desire, for example, to seek to use the power of the state to prevent the ending of a marriage, or to penalise birth outside wedlock; and not much more of an inclination to use voluntary institutional comment or ostracisms as a means of social control and punishment of one's fellow worshippers. What is left of formal 'establishment' is a source of occasional and cheerful embarrassment, not permanent strength, as the British – Christians and secularists alike – are, along with most Europeans, only too well aware of the dangers of the political embrace and of the morally dubious nature of the state: there are few Theocrats in either the Established or the other Christian Churches. The Church of England is, as Tim Winter (aka Abdal Hakim Murad) puts it, only 'dimly theocratic' and 'does not make the totalising claims which the radicals make for their own imams' (Seddon *et al.*, 2003: 20). (Note the qualification of 'radicals' slipped in.)

Furthermore, British Christians are liberal, in that they welcome the responsibility of running their own show. The 'blasphemy laws' (such as they are or were) may be a source of minor irritation to secularists, but the latter are in no way restrained or oppressed by these laws; and the laws, when attempts are made to conjure them into life, are a source of some amusement and embarrassment to religious leaders and their flocks. *Jerry Springer: The Opera*, playing at the Theatre Royal in Newcastle, attracted a tiny, amiable and generally inept Christian demonstration. The High Court threw out an attempt to use the blasphemy laws to have the show banned; and indeed it is the blasphemy laws themselves that have now shuffled off the stage. In Newcastle, the launch of the *Da Vinci Code* (a tedious novel and even more tedious film, in which, among other things, Christ allegedly breeds with Mary Magdalene) prompted a diocesan discussion 'event' – which, by some odd Anglican reasoning, took place at one of Newcastle's squalid night clubs. There, in the semi-surreptitious semi-gloom of a normally more lively place, two bishops, a Methodist lecturer, a Catholic nun and an assembly of Christians concluded that, however much the book offended, so long as Jesus was being talked about, that was fine: 'so long as Jesus was being talked about' would appear to be an encouragement *to* blasphemy, rather than an abjuration *of* it. However, no Christian called for the burning of the book, the film or the author. Providing another occasion for offence, a statue of Jesus with an erect penis was, in 2007, put on show at the Baltic Centre for Contemporary Art (*sic*), on the Gateshead side of the River Tyne. A Mr Michael Phillips, from the Christian Legal Centre, Reading, wrote to *The Times* claiming that 'many Christians demonstrated against this and the strength of feelings ran high. Many expressed their desire to destroy the statue, but desisted, knowing this not to be lawful' (*Times*, 5 March 2008). Mr Phillips wistfully commented that the Northumbria Police showed no interest in the matter. Perhaps the police, too, felt that the Church was well protected *so long as Jesus was being talked about*. Few Christians I know would feel that their religion was being well served by state-enforced censorship, let alone by riot and uproar, visiting death and death threats on makers of blasphemously erect penises or writers of novelistic profanities, or the drawers of cartoons or the baptisers of teddy bears. Some of my co-religionists may be happy to note that the Baltic Centre for Contemporary Art is now in serious financial difficulties – punishment enough, perhaps, and clear evidence of that firm Anglican dogma: that God is big enough to look after himself. British Christianity is moderate, a religion that facilitates engagement with a liberal, pluralist society, rather than seeking to inhibit it.

Moderate Muslims should not, looking at all this, assume, with Ms Dadabhoy (see above), that our tolerance is a form of religious idiocy.

British religion, predominantly Christian, predominantly Anglican, is paradoxically best understood through a secular poem, Philip Larkin's 'Church Going'. The secular or agnostic Larkin, on a cycling trip, wanders into an empty church. Larkin knows that he is in a church, and 'in awkward reverence' he takes off his bicycle clips, though he also comments that 'the place was not worth stopping for'. Larkin's description of the sad dilapidation of the building and its accoutrements is only too familiar to the average church visitor. Larkin describes the paraphernalia of church ritual lying about; and these are clearly, if residually, familiar to him. Noting that this 'empty shell' (the church) will probably become incomprehensible to later generations, he asks 'what remains when disbelief has gone?' There are, that is, those who believe (or believed) in what the church stood for; those who (like him) consciously choose to disagree with what it stood for – they 'disbelieve'; and then, if the decayed state of the building is any indication, there will be those who neither believe nor disbelieve, but for whom the place is simply incomprehensible and irrelevant. They will see no more reason for taking off their bicycle clips than if they were in WH Smith or Woolworths. With little sense that he is doing much more than hanging on to a disappearing tradition, Larkin concludes by saying of the building that:

> A serious house on serious earth it is,
> In whose blent air all our compulsions meet,
> Are recognised, and robed as destinies.
> And that much never can be obsolete,
> Since someone will forever be surprising
> A hunger in himself to be more serious,
> And gravitating with it to this ground,
> Which, he once heard, was proper to grow wise in,
> If only that so many dead lie round.

British religion is as much architecture as theology; more liturgy than dogma; a form of lively and profound nostalgia, with a doubtful and jaunty future. And as such it is much to be recommended. Its future is probably best guaranteed (if at all) precisely because it shares with its historical rival, atheism or agnosticism, a full subscription to the values of liberty. For that reason, its ritual and theology are in a bit of a mess. Crucially, we have little anticipation that our children will 'naturally' be Christian – we may, and do, hope; and we have absolutely *no desire at all* to somehow *make* them, compulsorily, members of the Church. There are no bars to 'apostasy', no need to appeal to either canonical scripture or authoritative tradition, to demonstrate a very profound indifference to compulsion. We have fond and serious memories of our saints and martyrs, of the many men and women on 'our side' who were wrong, and of the many men and women on the 'other' and bitterly resented 'side' who turned out to be right. The quarrels are over. There is no anger in the nostalgia – and men and women, astonishingly enough, actually pray and worship together.

The Christian Church has another moderate strength, well indicated by Larkin's last line. There are thousands of churches, large and small, ornate and crude, opulent and dilapidated, scattered around Britain, visited or seen by many millions of people who *know them for what they are* because our dead (*our* dead) lie in and around them, 'robed as destinies'. Complementing the churches are the tens of thousands of public monuments, buildings and (especially) war memorials – the 20th century's main and most prominent innovation in religious architecture – proclaiming, in location, epigraphy and design, the story of the nation, its religion, its wars, its dead and our involvement with them. The religion is enmeshed with the nation, with neither being warped by the other; and they are both wrapped in the sense of the succession of generations to which Larkin refers. Christianity in general, and the Church of England in particular, is part of the history of the nation, and the nation is part of the history of the Church. And both Church and nation are lower-case liberal, moderate to the core. One of the Prefaces to *The Book of Common Prayer* sets this out very precisely:

> We condemn no other nations, nor prescribe any thing
> but to our own people only, for we think it convenient
> that every country should use such ceremonies as they
> think best to the setting forth of God's honour and
> glory, and to the reducing of the people to a most
> perfect and godly living, without error or superstition;
> and that they should put away other things, which from
> time to time they perceive to be most abused, as in
> men's ordinances it often chanceth diversely in divers
> countries.

That such an understanding of the autochthonous place of religion in society makes sense even to outsiders was well illustrated by the delicious discomfiture experienced by the Muslim academic Tariq Modood, when, in 1996/97, he convened a collocation on the 'established' nature of the Church of England. To his evident surprise, none of the spokespersons for minority religions wanted anything to do with 'dis-establishment'; the Buddhist, for example, saying that 'In Britain today we are in the happy position where the state impinges very little on the religious life of its citizens' (see Davies, 2007: 92). Moderate Muslims should not, on hearing such news, simply urge upon us the demand for more and more freedom for themselves. They should first of all note that neither they nor their religion has played any part *whatsoever* in arriving at this 'happy position'; and then they should ask themselves whether their demands for *their* religion, and its nature as practised, are compatible with the maintenance of the liberties we here have, with such difficulty, won over so long a time. In asking this, they should most definitely look at the nature of the states and societies in which Islam is dominant. These I have presented in Chapter 4 above. 'How is it', asks Yasmin Alibhai-Brown, chairwoman of British Muslims for Secular Democracy, 'that Sikhs and Hindus can live in a democracy but not Muslims?' (*Guardian*, 2 May 2008). Perhaps the answer can be found in sex, to which I now turn.

CHAPTER 7

AGONY AUNTS: LOVE, SEX AND MARRIAGE

The journal *India Today* quite regularly publishes sample surveys of young (18–35) urban Indians, the 'YIPPIES', i.e. 'Young Indian People with Influence'. Some 70 per cent of India's population is under 34. These are the most modern of the country's steadily expanding middle class, and are mostly Hindus (like the majority of India's billion-plus people). A 2006 survey found that 75 per cent of them were against 'sex before marriage', including 93 per cent of women. It would seem that 'sex before marriage' meant precisely that – the pollsters did not ask about sex *without* marriage! Some 70 per cent were against 'staying with the person you love before marriage' (i.e. they were opposed to cohabitation before marriage); 75 per cent felt that arranged marriages were best; 70 per cent would not change their religion in order to marry the person they loved (males and females did not differ in their opinion on this); 68 per cent would prefer to live in a joint – multigenerational – rather than a nuclear, family, though this option was less popular with women (66 per cent) than with men (70 per cent); 57 per cent of men had watched porn, as compared with 13 per cent of women (35 per cent overall). The 2005 poll found similarly high levels of support for arranged marriages and the rejection of cohabitation before marriage; 88 per cent opposed kissing in public; 70 per cent of young Indians would not countenance placing their elderly relatives in an old people's home, and a similar number preferred the idea of a joint family to that of a nuclear one; 78 per cent had never dieted to look slim and fashionable. Some 71 per cent went to a place of worship either daily or weekly and 66 per cent fasted for religious reasons. The 2007 poll elicited the fact that 95 per cent would not smoke or drink in front of their parents and that 70 per cent were against co-education. The same percentage (70 per cent) thought that love marriages were more successful than arranged ones – presumably, given the equally high level of support for arranged marriages, they had in mind a sensible compromise between the two modes of forming a marital union! All three polls showed substantial majorities for a 'unified religious code for all religions in India', by which they meant that no one religion should be privileged, and that India's 'socialist secular democratic Republic' should treat religion as a 'private' sphere, with equal freedom for all. Every poll gave substantial majorities willing to join the armed forces should India find itself at war – something that has, of course, happened within their young lifetimes and could well happen again.

Most of these young people will, of course, be Hindus, rather than Muslims, and are (obviously) living in India, not Great Britain. But I start this chapter on sex and marriage with India's Hindus to make two points. First, Muslims are not alone in living within a very conservative sexual or gender regime: so do most Hindus. Second, it is undoubtedly the West that is 'immoderate', and the apparent conservatism of Muslims is much closer both to the historical norm and to much non-Western contemporary sexual culture. Romantic marriage, for example, embarked on by two young, inexperienced, star-struck lovers, began (as Larkin almost put it) to happen only in 1961. And, after a very short period of supremacy, this model is now disappearing. Apart from this brief period in the West, marriages have always been arranged, and arranged for broad extrinsic kin and communal interests, and not to gratify the lusts and fancies of the young (such fancies having always, as Romeo and Juliet found out, been a dangerous nuisance). Marriage and procreation have always been regulated: regulated by the old and not by the young; by males and not by females. Regulated to buttress communal solidarity, to control the accumulation and transmission of wealth and property, and, crucially, to maximise the degree of congruency between the genetic and the cultural identities and resources of the group. The more vulnerable are the gene pool and the culture – on account of, for example, migration and the concomitant presence of Others (including sexually available Others) – the more rigidly enforced is likely to be the system of rules that tries to tie genes and culture together. The fact that any one human being can readily mate with any other makes this business more, rather than less, urgent. Nothing so decides and advertises the collapse of a culture or society as exogamy.

For better or worse, Muslims resident in Britain stand four-square within an ancient, conservative tradition of sexual regulation – a tradition *designed primarily to serve the material interests of the natal community* and not the amatory appetites of the young or, indeed, the interests of any broader community. At times, this leads to the institution and tolerance of what, to us, are impermissibly strict and even punitive practices, and I shall deal with things like cousin marriage, arranged marriage, coerced marriage, female genital mutilation and 'honour' (what honour?) killing later in this chapter (having wondered initially whether to deal with the last three of those things in Chapter 5, under the section on Terror).

AGONY AUNTS

I will attend first to what seems to me to be a peculiarity of the Muslim sexual regimen, i.e. its grounding in an extraordinarily detailed *religious* code, with or without 'ethnic' variations. The physical body is mapped by religious texts, themselves rendered authoritative and prescriptive by reference to the prophet Muhammad. An example: on the Muslim website Pink Islam (accessed 15 May 2008), we find a discussion about a Muhammad-approved method of shaving pubic hair:

> Removing pubic hair is one of the parts of the *fitrah* (natural disposition). The Messenger of Allah (*sallallaahu alayi wa sallam*) has said: 'The fitrah

consists of five things: circumcision, trimming the
moustache, cutting the nails, plucking the armpit hairs
and shaving the pubic hairs' (Al-Bukhari and Muslim)...
Shaving: attention First Timers! The pubic area is
sensitive and may take time to adjust to the razor.
Don't worry about a smooth shave the first month...

And so on. As an aside, I should point out here that
Al-Bukhari and Muslim are two authoritative compilers of
hadith, the reputed sayings of Muhammad, which carry
canonical (though frequently debated) status. These writings
are very numerous – and contested: the Turkish government,
in its design for a moderate Islam, is currently engaged in a
project to reduce them from 160,000 to 10,000 (Daniel Pipes
website, 22 May 2008). Tim Winter's Sunna Project hopes to
have the job 'substantially fulfilled after several decades',
though it takes no responsibility for the use to which they may
then be put (Sunna Project website, February 2002).
Meanwhile, of course, the very superabundance of such
'authoritative' texts provides ample scope for their application to anything and everything. For non-Muslims, advice on
such matters as pubic hair and other bodily matters is more
readily, if just as confusingly, available on Western websites
and in countless 'women's magazines' (and, for men, in magazines such as *Men's Health*, which I read from time to time).
Such texts lack canonical status.

What is distinctive about the Muslim prescription is that
it is embroidered into (or onto) the life and sayings of
Muhammad, the 'Messenger of God'. Where in the Christian
world would anyone, even the most rigorous fundamentalist,
think to invoke either the example or the words of Jesus on
the matter of shaving pubic hair? What credence, if any, could
such invocations expect? Furthermore, whereas contemporary Western sexology is secular and all about issuing *permission* and advice, Muslim sexology is about prescription,
proscription and control. Whereas sexual matters in the West
are now referred to secular sexologists and psychologists
(who see in repression nothing but bad), Muslims will tend to

seek (and will certainly be offered) first (though not only) the prescriptive religious text, preferably one derived from the sayings of Muhammad.

Another example:

> I have been engaged for a long time, I've also been alone with my fiancée I want to hold her hands but am not sure if I should, my question to you is what are the ruling on touching one's fiancée or being alone with her.
>
> *Muslim Weekly*, 10–16 June 2005

'Sister Sabia', the lifestyle 'Agony Aunt' for the English-language newspaper, the *Muslim Weekly*, replied, stating that

> ibn Qudaamah said: 'It is not permitted for him to be alone with her, because she is forbidden and Islam only allows him to look, thus khulwah (being alone with her) remains forbidden, and because there is no certainty that nothing forbidden will take place if he is alone, as the Prophet (swa) said: 'no man is alone with a woman, but the *Shaytan* (Satan) is the third one present'. He should not look at her in a lustful or suspicious manner. Ahmad said, in a report narrated by Saalih, 'he may look at the face, but not in a lustful manner'.
>
> *ibid.*

Another inquirer wanted some exegetical detail of the Prophet's *hadith* allowing a man to look at a woman before deciding whether or not to marry her (the term 'non-*mahram*' means that the woman in question is non-kin, and therefore marriageable):

> What exactly is the person allowed to see exactly? Is he allowed to see her hair (entire head)? Sister says: Islam commands us to lower our gaze and forbids looking at non-mahram women. This is in order to purify people's souls and protect their honor. There are, however, certain exceptions in which it is permissible to look at a

non-mahram woman for reasons of necessity, one of
which is the case of proposing marriage... From Abu
Hurayrah: 'I was with the Prophet (swa) when a man
came to him and told him that he had married a woman
of the Ansaar. The Messenger of Allah (swa) said to
him, "have you seen her?" He said "No". He said, "go
and look at her, for there is something in the eyes of the
Ansaar"' (Reported by Muslim, no. 1424; and by al-
Daaraqutni, 3/253 (34)).

ibid.

This story is repeated in a 1997 book by Dr Yusuf al-
Qaradawi. Dr al-Qaradawi comments that Muhammad's
comment about the eyes of the Ansaar woman was a reference
to a possible defect in the eye. He tells the story of Al-
Mughira ibn Shu'bah:

> I asked for a woman in marriage and Allah's Messenger
> – peace be upon him – asked me whether I had looked
> at her. When I replied that I had not, he said, 'Then
> look at her, for it may produce love between you'. I
> went to her parents and informed them of the Prophet's
> advice. They seemed to disapprove of the idea. Their
> daughter heard the conversation from her room and
> said, 'If the Prophet – peace be upon him – has told you
> to look at me, then look'. I looked at her, and
> subsequently I married her.
>
> al-Qaradawi, 1997: 229–30

Al-Qaradawi embroiders this discussion of the views of
Muhammad with the touching story of Jarir ibn Abdullah,
who said about his wife that 'Before marriage I used to hide
under a tree to see her' (*ibid.*).

There is something to be said for such shyness: four
hours after I wrote this, while I was travelling in the middle
of the day on the Tyne and Wear Metro, I found myself
sitting opposite a young Geordie couple. The girl, sitting not
four feet from me, quite casually and with no preamble or

'foreplay' whatsoever, reached into her boyfriend's trousers and began to fumble with his crotch. I got off at the next stop, so I have no idea how far this went. One wonders what on earth Agony Aunt Sabia – or indeed, my wife's Aunt Esther – would have said or done if confronted by such full frontal popular culture of this type. But perhaps the young couple were, in fact, married.

Naved Siddiqi, a founder of *Emel*, a Muslim lifestyle magazine that 'celebrates contemporary British Muslim culture', told the BBC's Linda Serck that the very concept of a Muslim 'lifestyle' magazine was a problem, as 'Lifestyle magazines tend to have an obsession with things that don't sit comfortably with belief in God.' As Mr Siddiqi explained, 'a typical lifestyle magazine would have features and images with an unhealthy obsession with sex and women'. Mr Siddiqi, who, at the time, was president of the Berkshire branch of the Islamic Society of Britain, said that *Emel* 'overcame the "sex sells" dilemma by, for example, featuring fashion without the models, instead displaying modern garments on hangers and on grassy lawns... It worked, and female readers who were *not* Muslim wrote in to say how refreshing the approach was' (Serck, 2004).

An alternative approach was available in *Reveal* magazine, a fairly typical glossy 'young' production. *Reveal* magazine has an 'agony' page presided over by Marina 'She's a Shocker!' Gask, an 'X-Rated Agony Aunt (Life, Love and Sex)', who answers the 'questions no one else dares' (*Reveal* 11, 15–21 March 2008). To help her, she has a male assistant, Dominic 'Sex Spot Sex is a Beauty Treatment' Utton. Dominic provides a 'Bloke's View' on a question sent in to the magazine:

Me and my girlfriend are both virgins and we are planning to sleep together. She is on the Pill and I would prefer not to use a condom as I've read that they restrict pleasure. As neither of us have ever had sex before, does that mean that there is no chance of having an STD? I want it to be perfect, but is it safe to have unprotected sex?

Dominic: Use condoms – Yes, they're fiddly and awkward, and can involve a frustrating pause in the action, but these days they're also a necessity. Don't be disheartened, however – many brands are sensitive enough not to restrict your pleasure. By letting your girlfriend put it on you, you can even add something to the whole experience!

Magazines of this type are full of urgings to have sex – as well as advertising for and of sex: 'FREE HOT SEXY LIVE TALKS' or 'Sex Position of the Week: The Kneeling Dog – fed up with lying on your back? Try this for a change'. A couple of articulated mannequins illustrate the 'Kneeling Dog Position' (*ibid.*).

Sugar Lad Mag for April 2008 ('It's all about him – for you') offers a

Kissing Class, your expert guide to professional pashing, yum! Find a partner you've snogged before – ideal to practice on...after approx 15 seconds slow right down then gently glide your tongue along his lips...and so on.

To be fair, there are some criticisms of all this – from 14 (14!)-year-old Chibuco Beardmore of Yorkshire, who disliked the idea of 'serial snogging...yuck – why lock lips with total randoms one after the other?' (*ibid.*).

Indeed, Chibuco.

Dominic 'Sex Spot' Utton of *Reveal* would presumably have little to say in support of a letter writer to the *Muslim Weekly*, who was 'duly unsettled' by an NHS television advertisement about safe sex:

It seems that society has accepted that everyone is fornicating randomly and there is nothing that can be done about it but to remind all to have sex safely and responsibility! This erosion of moral values is a very serious and sad thing. Sexual liberation is naught but Satan's deception. Fornicating only cheapens the parties

involved and screws their minds and self esteems [*sic*].
Who seriously wakes up the next morning feeling great
after a one night stand?... Pick up the Qur'an, Allah
will guide you right.

Samsuddin ibn Rias Uddin,
Muslim Weekly, 22 February 2008

Perhaps Mr Uddin is right: in the *Weekend* magazine of
the *Sunday Telegraph* of 15 March 2008, we find a letter from
a 30-year-old man saying that he had

started seeing a woman in her early 50s. [She] is
fantastically sexy... I'm falling for her, but I feel a bit
used generally. She seems to want me only for sex and
to have no interest in me as a person. She boots me out
at 1am.

(Answer): The attraction of a younger man could be
making her excited. Women get giggly when they are
excited and infatuated...this is not about you but about
the vanity of an ageing woman in lust.

Here, in the sneer at the sexual 'vanity of an ageing
woman in lust', we perhaps see a typically *Telegraph* reten-
tion of a residuum of what was once a major feature of most
systems of sexual control, Muslim or otherwise: the tendency
to locate the greater weight of their prescriptions, expectations and strictures on women. Muslims retain a lot more of
this system than is now to be found in the West. True, men
are also under the rule of the Messenger of Allah, who, for
example and according to Ma'qal ibn Yasar, said: 'It is better
for one of you to be pricked in the head with an iron pick
than to touch a woman whom it is unlawful to touch' (al-
Qaradawi, 1997: 217). This is reported as a *hadith* of al-
Tabarani – 'whose transmitters are authentic and sound' – as
well as of al-Bahhaqi. The book from which I take these
quotes, *The Lawful and the Prohibited in Islam,* is distributed
free by the Al-Birr Foundation of London, and its every

comment on sexual matters is footnoted and referenced to the sayings of Muhammad, the Qur'an and the *hadith*. Chapter 3, 'Marriage and Family Life', is concerned with the details of the rules about the female body and female sexuality. We learn, for example, that women wearing revealing clothes are regarded as 'naked', and 'The Prophet – pbuh – has informed us that among the dwellers of hell are such women as are clothed, yet naked, seduced and being seduced. These shall not enter the Garden, nor shall (even) its fragrance reach them' (*ibid.*: 217).

As I said above (Chapter 3), Muslims have always found themselves surrounded by non-Muslims, and their sexual codes, as with their other codes, both identify the worrying (tempting, dangerous) presence of the Other, and use this presence to give sharp(er) focus to Muslim distinctiveness. Al-Qaradawi quotes a *hadith* by Umm Samah, in which, while discussing same-sex use of public baths, the prophet Muhammad prohibits undressing even there: 'If a woman takes off her clothes outside her own house, Allah will tear His covering from her' (*ibid.*: 214). Al-Qaradawi comments:

> When Islam takes such a strict view of women's entering public baths which are, after all, buildings with four walls in which only women are allowed, imagine its judgement concerning the nearly-nude women lying about on beaches and the swimming pool, exposing their nakedness to the hungry and lustful eyes of every passerby without any sense of shame. Assuredly they have torn down every veil between themselves and their most Merciful Lord. And their men are partners in their sin, since they are responsible protectors of their women. If only they knew!
>
> *ibid.*

Again, the major onus for maintaining communal boundaries falls on women, as the above and the following examples make clear. It should, of course, always be borne in mind that, as the opening paragraph of this chapter shows, cultures and religions other than Islam are also considerably less permissive than we are. This, of course, in no way diminishes the fact that Muslims are preoccupied with the control of the detail of sex and gender relationships.

In March 2008, the *Islamic Times* answered a question about dancing at weddings, saying that other than within the boundaries of *mahram* (i.e. family relationships), 'mixing with both genders is not allowed in Islam', and that 'whatever excites passion opens ways for illicit sexual relations between a man and a woman and promotes indecency and obscenity is *haraam* (forbidden)'. This conclusion had been preceded by a statement that

> under no circumstance may men and women dance together as this is absolutely haraam. The reason behind this prohibition is that with mixed dancing bodily contact is close and improper sexual desires are aroused. This has been strictly forbidden by Islam in an attempt to block the way against evil. Another important point is that in all cases where there is dancing and it happens to be accompanied by music, the music should be acceptable to Islam, whereby the content of the song should not be against the morals and teachings of Islam and it should be without certain instruments, as the Holy Prophet Muhammad-ur Rasullullaah (Sallallaahu Alayhi Wasallam) mentions, 'There will be people from my Ummah who will seek to make lawful fornication, wearing of silk, wine and the use of musical instruments' (Bukhaari vol 2 pg 837). In another Hadith, Rasullullaah (Sallallaahu Alayhi Wasallam) states 'A group of my Ummah will drink wine calling it by other than its real name. Joyous will be made for them through the playing of musical instruments and by the singing of females. Allah Taa'la will cleave the earth under them and turn them into apes and pigs' (Abu Dawood vol 2 pg 519).
>
> *Islamic Times*, 10 March 2008

There is much discussion in Islam about the *'awrah*, the part of the male and female body that is not to be shown – see, for example, Qur'an Surah 24, 31; and Pink Islam website, accessed 11 March 2008. There is, as usual, considerable exegetical debate on this topic; but the general drift is very clear: the display of bodies, especially women's bodies, in anything other than the marital home is very carefully controlled. There is, of course, little need to comment that, for totally opposite reasons, it is precisely the display of the female *'awrah* that so preoccupies many magazines on sale in British newsagents and other less reputable places.

From Fatima Mernissi's account of life in a Moroccan harem, it would seem that incarceration in the harem, with a (male) gatekeeper, was the favoured way of ensuring control over women, and she refers to the tragic end inevitably in store for any Arab woman who sought 'sensuous enjoyment, frivolous entertainment and happiness' outside the gated enclosure (Mernissi, 1995: 111–12). In *Fatwa: Living With a Death Threat* (2004), Jacky Trevane, an Englishwoman who married an Egyptian, soon found herself denied the right to leave the house and was savagely beaten, while pregnant, in order to preserve this aspect of male control. She was forced to flee back to England. 'A woman's place is in the home', while now a joke to us Westerners, is not so risible in Muslim (or indeed Hindu) communities. There is, on this matter, as on so many others, considerable play made by Muslim commentators with what seems to them to be the almost total lack of prescriptive concern on the part of their despised Western neighbours. In 2007, Umm Layth wrote 'Don't be ashamed of being a Muslimah':

> I don't understand why some of you sisters out there want to be just like the *kaafira*. Why would you want a life of ignorance when you are blessed with a life of simplicity and goodness? Why would you care what these *kuffar* women think about you, when it is you that should be thinking about how unlucky they are and making *du'aa* (prayer)? Why would you want to listen

to the music they listen to when you know it kills their heart? Why would you want to have boyfriends? Why would you want to discard your obligatory garments for trashy things that only prove you are desperate for attention? Why would you want to dress like a whore, smell like a whore, and act like a whore when you know their life is filthy? Why would you date a *kaafir* man and get pregnant and then expect Muslims to welcome you with open arms, and expect them to marry you off to a good Muslim man? It's your own damn fault that you end up in the messes you end up in. Grow up. Be thankful you have Islam and grab a hold of it. Stop calling yourself a *Muslimah* if you're going to be ashamed of being one. Because honestly, being a *Muslimah* is the best thing in the whole world. It's amazing. It's beautiful. And it makes life worth living.

Umm Layth blog, June–August 2007

There was a long correspondence about this – including a posting from a person saying not all non-Muslim women are filthy tramps; if they were, how would invitations to convert be successful? The writer instanced her mother, who, aged 75, became a Muslim: 'she was a good person before she became Muslim, Islam of course made her better'. Other correspondents criticised Umm Layth for the forcefulness of her language. Umm Layth defended herself, denying that she had said that all non-Muslim women were whores, and insisting on her views on perfume: 'in the Sunnah of our Beloved, he tells us not to wear perfume when going out'; in doing so, 'we are seriously disobeying Allah and his messenger'. This discussion continued, with questions being asked about the precise meaning of the particular *hadith*. One person wrote that the *hadith* referred to a prostitute who was motivated by

an intention other than of just smelling nice... If her intention is to use the fragrance to attract a male for the purpose of soliciting sexual business, then she is either a fornicator, an adulteress or both... If a woman goes to the *masjid* wearing a fragrance and she does not come in contact with men is there harm in it? Some women do come to the *masjid* with heavy scent of musk which is distracting to the prayers.

ibid.

Another contributor said that

Only Allah (swt) can judge each girls situation and struggles, and if a girl did go have a baby with her non-muslim boyfriend but repented sincerely, maybe she's a better muslims then all of us put together now, and who are we to say we are to marry off, whatever is her fate is written with Allah (swt). I think the way our communities (the Muslim American communities) judge girls so quickly based on the way the dress and every other outward quality is half of what is driving us nuts! [*sic* throughout]

On 7 August 2006, in a Channel 4 programme, *What Muslims Want*, a moderate Muslim taxi driver in Bolton gave, as one reason for his reversion to the faith and lifestyle of his fathers, the fact that the revealing dresses of women in Bolton (and the West in general?) meant that men would want 'to go and commit sexual acts *on* them' (my emphasis). Jon Snow, the presenter, ignored this extraordinary give-away, instead showing us several pictures of lubricious Bolton legs. The taxi driver was aware, if Mr Snow was not, that the more fragile or threatened (or tempted) the gene pool, the more insistent will be the demands for conformity to the cultural norms. There is no way that the women of Bolton will re-cover their legs. The taxi driver's only recourse is indeed to return to the 'faith and lifestyle' of his fathers, thus saving both him from committing sexual acts on Bolton's ladies, and them from having such sexual acts committed on them, by him.

Sonia Malik, of *Q-News*, a Muslim magazine, reported on female Muslim students at British universities: 'Girls Just Wanna Have Fun' (*Q-News*, no. 360, February 2005). As there are many young Muslim women in higher education (60,000 of the UK's 140,000 18–24-year-old Muslim women, according to the *Daily Mail* of 11 April 2005), this is quite a lot of fun. Ms Malik perhaps overstates matters when she describes such girls as caught between their 'despotic parents' and the 'wild days' at university; but she got closer to reality when she said that there was, in fact, more to British Islam's 'Bad Girls' than 'boys, booze and bhangra'. Nazia, a student from Bradford, said:

> At home we are constantly being subjected to tyrannical parents and hampered by endless rules which dictate our every move. University is the first and only chance a girl gets to lead her life exactly the way she wants it. Most Muslim girls don't even know what they want out of life when they first come here. They're not used to thinking for themselves or setting their own boundaries.

Other girls told Sonia about going wild for a bit, drinking, dating, dancing; one said 'you don't put your family reputation at risk if you are at university in a different city', while a medical student said:

> I have to live my whole life in the span of my five year degree because once I get back home, it's back to being constantly under my parents' thumb... My parents tried to make my older sister marry someone she didn't want to and she ran away. That meant that their grip over me tightened considerably. It is suffocating.

The reporter commented that most of the girls 'understood the importance of family honour', one girl saying that 'if upsetting your family or their honour means something to you, then you will never go too far'. Three of the girls interviewed by the *Daily Mail* all agreed that, after a 'free life' at university, they expected to have an arranged marriage and would keep their 'wild-child' days secret from their husbands. Interestingly, the *Q-News* article ended with the assurance that the names of all the interviewees had been changed 'to respect anonymity'.

Rendered anonymous, too, was 'Aisha Salim', a university student who, after several years of smoking, drinking and living with an English boyfriend, had recourse to a medical operation so as to 'restore' her virginity. (There are apparently operations to do this.) 'Aisha' was due to get married in Pakistan, where, to prove her virginity, she would be expected to hand over the traditional bloodstained wedding-night sheets:

> If my husband cannot prove to his family that I am a
> virgin, I would be hounded, ostracised and sent home in
> disgrace. My father, who is a devout Muslim, would
> regard it as the ultimate shame. The entire family could
> be cast out from friends and society they hold dear, and
> I honestly believe that one of my fanatically religious
> cousins or uncles might kill me in revenge.
> *Birmingham Eastern Voice*, 19–26 December 2007;
> *Daily Mail*, 17 December 2007

In April 2005, 'Sister Sabia' had to deal with a distressed woman whose husband reacted badly to their – mutual – discovery that she was not a virgin 'even though no one ever touched me before'. Sabia commented on the relative uselessness of the hymen as an indicator of virginity, and urged both the correspondent and her husband to remember the *hadith* (Muslim 5023) in which Muhammad warns about the capacity of the devil to cause division between husband and wife (*Muslim Weekly*, 8–14 April 2005). I cannot resist suggesting that Sabia might perhaps have drawn her correspondent's attention to Deuteronomy 22, 13–21.

Few of us Westerners are now too bothered about such things as hymens and virginity, or are familiar (or even comfortable) with the concept of 'family honour', though to be sure the concern is not totally absent from our minds. We have almost no tolerance of the idea that social or legal force or discipline, or even religious prescriptions, should be used to, say, control courtship activities or determine marital choice. We do, though, from time to time, in multicultural Britain, see its tragic side. Some years ago, we, unusually for the times, had a Muslim girl who came to my department at Newcastle University. Her father had not wanted her to go to university, and every night, from about 6pm onwards, he would telephone her on the hour, every hour, to ensure she was in her room (this was before mobile telephones). After some weeks of this, the girl disappeared. The father, weeping, came looking for his daughter. As far as I know, he never saw her again; we never did. One of Sonia Malik's respondents mentioned her elder sister, who ran away to escape an arranged marriage. Even though Ms Malik's interviewees were inevitably making compromises, and no doubt contrived to get on with their parents, there is little doubt that gender and generational relations between Muslims resident in Britain have a lot more in common with Mirpur and Sylhet than with us, if only because so many Muslim marriages are arranged across continents. Things are certainly changing, but there are counter-forces at work (such as the practice of inter-continental marriage).

Furthermore, an increasing body of evidence shows that this system, whatever its merits, carries a considerable weight of punitive control and duress, and, quite frequently, violence legitimated by religion. The issue is not 'just sex', but the systemic relationships between the identity of the community and the institution of male and parental power. Whether seen as community support or as community oppression, Muslim and other ethnic communities validate such power, and build it in to related practices such as cousin marriage, polygamy, arranged marriage, coerced marriage and female genital mutilation. Such social constructions become particularly problematic in the terrible business of 'honour' killing, and the grim things such practices tell us about the situation of Muslim women and Muslim communities in Great Britain.

When Fatima Mernissi (below) makes a point about polygamy, she is, in fact, making a point about this entire system of sex and gender management. She is discussing an event in 1992, when 1 million Moroccan women signed a petition against polygamy and divorce (i.e. the Muslim system by which men have both multiple wives and multiple divorces). 'An expert in Islamic religious sciences', spurred on by the fundamentalist press, issued a *fatwa* calling for the execution of the women (all of them?!) as heretics. Mernissi goes on:

> The fundamentalist press's defence of polygamy and divorce is in fact an attack against the right of women to participate in the law-making process. [Muslim governments] keep polygamy in the family law codes, not because it is widespread but because they want to show women that their needs are not important. The law is not there to serve them, nor guarantee their right to happiness and emotional security. The prevailing belief is that women and the law do not belong together, women ought to accept men's law because they cannot change it. The suppression of a man's right to polygamy would mean that women have a say in the law, that society is not run by and for men's whims alone. Where a Muslim government stands on the question of polygamy is a good way to measure the degree to which it has accepted democratic ideas.
>
> Mernissi, 1995: 38

The incidence of polygamy in Britain, where it is illegal, is small – as far as we know, a thousand or so, mostly Muslim, families are constructed in that way (*Muslim Weekly*, 8 February 2008). Polygamy is, however, part of a much wider system of marriage 'management', in which Muslim communities resident here have a very distinctive way of structuring male/female relationships and the production of children. The 'key variable' is 'endogamy', i.e. the insistence that marriages take place *within* a defined collectivity; that this exclusivist system should be formally defined and heavily enforced; and that deviation should be punished. The strength of endogamy among Muslims is indicated by Samad and Eade's figures, which show that, whereas 20 per cent of Afro-Caribbean, 17 per cent of Chinese and 4 per cent of Indian people are either married to or living with a white person, this is true of only 1 per cent of Bangladeshis and Pakistanis (Samad and Eade, 2002: 29).

To maintain this system, arranged marriage is widely accepted and widely practised among Muslims living in Britain. Samad and Eade, using 1997 data from Modood and Berthoud, show that in Pakistani and Bangladeshi communities, in the majority of cases, parents 'made the decision' about marriage, either on their own or with their children being allowed 'a say'. Among Pakistanis aged 35+, the actual figure was 75 per cent; for Pakistanis aged 16–34, it was 65 per cent; for Bangladeshis aged 35 and over – 64 per cent; and for those aged 16–34 – 50 per cent. 'Making the decision on their own' accounts for 16 per cent of all Pakistani marriages and 21 per cent of Bangladeshi marriages (interestingly, older Bangladeshis were, at 13 per cent, the most likely to have taken the decision on their own – compared with 8 per cent for all the other groups).

How this all 'works out' in terms of human happiness or misery is a mystery, and will probably remain so for the foreseeable future; there are far fewer divorces in Muslim society, but we do not know if this indicates a better way of life or simply the power of 'the system'. What we do know, however, is that it creates and consolidates major cultural barriers between us and Muslims, making the (universally?) desired integration that much more difficult to achieve. Even (or especially?) people for whom the system has not, first time around, worked well would seem determined to operate within its parameters. In 2007, the *Muslim Weekly* matrimonial page – 'Men Seeking Brides-to-be, Women Seeking Grooms-to-be' – printed a letter from a

British Muslim Bangladeshi Female single parent, divorced from an incompatible arrange marriage abroad, age 32, 5 feet 5 inch, medium build from a respectable family. Seeking a kind faithful honest hard-working trustworthy British Muslim brother for any race who can provide protection, guidance, love and maintain a family and share responsibilities, be a friend, companion, husband, provider, photo would be appreciated for physical compatibility.

Muslim Weekly, 27–30 November 2007

She is, of course, self-arranging her own (second) marriage, the first arranged one having failed; but the sought-after new marriage has to be within the religious culture that arranged the first one: 'any race' will do, but the man must definitely be a 'trustworthy British Muslim'.

There is, of course, a systemic connection between arranged and coerced marriage; and while Samad and Eade are unable to provide figures for this, they do suggest that the 'media' figure of about 1,000 coerced marriages a year is correct, the vast majority of these involving women being coerced into marriage with men not of their own choosing. *The Times* (12 March 2008) quoted a study of Luton, whose author took the view that there were probably 4,000 coerced marriages a year in the UK. The *Daily Telegraph* of 24 January 2008 quoted Judge Marilyn Mornington, who said that official statistics on forced marriage gave but the 'tip of the iceberg'. She called for a campaign in media and schools 'in the hope of changing attitudes in communities of Asian origin'. 'We have to remember', said Judge Mornington, 'that, even with these distressing figures, the vast majority of the Asian population and the other groups that practise forced marriage feel equally abhorrent as we do towards these practices. But it is a very difficult area that we need to tackle.' In this she would have had the support of Dr Ghayasuddin Siddiqui, who said that '80% or over of our people come from a rural background, it would take time before they began to feel at ease with their new environment and be able to contribute to the wider society with what they can derive from their own Islamic heritage' (*Muslim Weekly*, 18–24 March 2004). The government has recently brought in the

Forced Marriage (Civil Protection) Act, Justice Minister Bridget Prentice saying that 'Forced marriage is an appalling and indefensible practice that the Government is working hard to stop.' She said the Act would go a long way to ensuring that young men and women and children would not be forced into marriage against their will, and that those already in such marriages would receive protection (Ministry of Justice website, 27 March 2008).

'Honour killing' is perhaps the most horrific feature of this treatment of women. While it is not restricted to Muslims, they are regularly involved in it. I have to say that I can see no way in which 'honour' is an appropriate adjective to apply to what is nothing short of murder. In *Crimes of the Community: Honour-Based Violence in the UK*, James Brandon and Salam Hafez deal with forced marriage, domestic violence, 'honour' killing (the demurring commas are mine) and female genital mutilation. As with the section on Terror in Chapter 5, there is little need to dwell on the dreadfulness of all these practices. Instead, we can leave it to Brandon and Hafez to point out that such killings are not just more examples of 'ordinary' domestic violence or 'crimes of passion':

> While typical incidents of domestic violence involve men using force against their own wives, honour-based abuses regularly involve a woman's own sons, brothers and sisters, as well as members of their extended family and in-laws. Similarly, the pre-planned and ritualised nature of this violence (particularly in the case of honour-killings and female genital mutilation) makes such behaviour distinct from other ad-hoc forms of violence against women... Many British women, and indeed many men, are told they are not allowed to be independent, to have control over their own bodies [or] an opportunity to choose their own destiny.
>
> Brandon and Hafez, 2008: 2

As with so much of this subject, hard data are difficult to come by. The authors of *Crimes of the Community* quote police figures, which give an average of 10–12 women killed every year, while the *Yorkshire Post*, to which Brandon and Hafez also refer, claims that the figure is 13 women *a day* (*ibid.*: 37). (I assume the *Yorkshire Post* is referring not just to the UK.) In Pakistan itself, up to 1,000 women are 'honour' killed every year, and in Bangladesh there are 'several hundred', plus 'accidents' and (real) suicides. If, to all of this, we add female infanticide, the abortion of female foetuses and the practice of giving girls less food than boys, then, as Brandon and Hafez point out, we have a major part of the explanation for why, in Bangladesh, there are 105 men for every 100 women, even though so many men migrate (*ibid.*: 41). An increasing amount of data (Anand and Cochrane, 2005; Bhugra *et al.*, 1999) indicates growing distress (suicide, attempted suicide, depression, self-harm) among young Asian women in the UK. Bhugra reports that the attempted suicide rate among young Asian women is 2.5 times that for white women and seven times that for Asian men (Bhugra *et al.*, 1999). Brandon and Hafez provide figures for female genital mutilation in England and Wales, which show that, by 2007, 65,000 women had undergone some form of this reprehensible treatment. In 2007, there were 16,000 girls under the age of 15 who had undergone (or were at risk of) type III circumcision, i.e. infibulation (Brandon and Hafez, 2008: 70).

Brandon and Hafez print one story, which seems to me to tell us quite enough about this:

In April 2005 Samira Nazir, a 25 year old Muslim woman, was killed in her family home in Southall, London, by her brother, Azhar Nazir, and her cousin after she refused to marry any of the men proposed to her by her family. When her family told her she would have to marry a man of their choice, she replied that she wanted to marry her Afghan boyfriend and threatened to leave home, saying to her mother 'You are not my mother anymore'. Her brother and cousin then held her down, stabbed her 17 times and cut her throat. They then forced her two sisters – aged two and four – to watch her die. As her brother was led away by police he told them 'there had been a problem with my sister. She does not wish to have an arranged marriage. We only allow marriage within the family. My sister wanted to run away from the house and was stopped.'

ibid.: 50

She was indeed stopped. May the Lord bless and keep her.

In my last chapter, I attempt to get away from such savageries, and to see if there may be some room for optimism in the writings of a group of 'self-defined' Moderate Muslims.

CHAPTER 8

INNOCENTS OF ISLAM, PIOUS HOPES OF THE WEST

Muslims are often asked why their faith does not get modern or undergo liberalisation. Such a question shows a misunderstanding of Islam and its relationship to modernity. As a phenomenon essentially of the Christian world, modernity has not affected the Muslim world to the same extent. The impact of the Enlightenment in Europe culminated in a separation between faith and reason. Secularisation publicly elevated the profane and relegated religion to the realm of the private.

Mohammad Siddique Seddon, Islam for Today website, accessed 12 May 2008

A summary: I have felt it necessary to argue that, while 'Moderate Muslims' may well exist in large numbers, they have not been tried and tested, not shown to be effective. Claims for their dominance in, and control over, the Muslim 'community' are just that – claims; they are 'not proven', to use the sensible Scottish legal formula. *Per contra*, of course, Muslim terrorism is most graphically and definitely 'proven' – its potency being in evidence, for example, every time you try to get on an aeroplane and have to struggle to take off your shoes or are forced to abandon an innocent tube of toothpaste. Muslim terror is a quotidian experience. To date, the response of Moderate Muslims (and British liberal apologists) has been to deny this, to insist that terror is 'not Islamic'; that those Muslims who are clearly murderously inclined are 'not' Muslims; and/or that, even if terrorism does in fact exist within their ranks, then it is all due to the depredations and iniquities of the West – over many centuries and to this day. So the West had it coming. There are, of course, huge confusions in each and every one of these declarations.

Beyond the 'terror thing', there are, as I hope I have demonstrated, very clear, very considerable and, sadly, in many ways growing social and cultural differences between people like me (and my friends) and the great majority of ordinary Muslims. In that sense at least, 'moderate' does not mean the same thing in Muslim Bradford (Muslim Bradford?!) as it does in, say, middle-class Gosforth, Newcastle upon Tyne, where I and many of my friends live. Things do, however, seem to be changing in the direction of a little more openness: Muslims such as Ed Husain (quoted at the beginning of Chapter 5's section on Terror) seem to accept that 'default' violence is as Muslim as *halal* meat. At the time of writing, several individuals and organisations are putting themselves forward as – or as representing – Moderate Muslims, willing (often at some risk to themselves) to face up to the association of Muslim with terror, and to become 'part' of the West by trying to work out how their version of Islam might best address the traditions and concerns of Westerners. Necessarily, therefore, this involves the moderate Muslim exegete in an imagined or real 'conversation', articulated or not, with his putative (or even real) non-Muslim equivalents and interlocutors. This Moderate Muslim will seek to address what he or she considers to be the major moral, philosophical and theological concerns and beliefs of these conjectural Western interlocutors.

In this concluding chapter, I make what is perhaps my major point: that it is precisely in these attempts at moderate 'conversations' with moderate Westerners that the limitations of Moderate Muslims become clear. These eminently moderate and often scholarly men (nearly always men) have difficulty, as we shall see, in getting out from under the weight of the 'philosophy of history', the Muslim meta-narrative that they have inherited. Their essential 'house style' is to seek accommodation with the West on the basis of a contrived (if convenient) reinterpretation (or misrepresentation) of what the West is, leaving Islam pretty much unsullied and intact.

I can only assume that this tactic (if tactic it be) is primarily the result of the anticipated minatory intractability of some of their brother Muslim interlocutors whom they might also be addressing, or who might simply be 'listening in'. Such a three-way conversation must be difficult to manage. It is also difficult to render plausible.

Moderate Muslims appear in a variety of contexts and publications.

T. J. Winter is a university lecturer in Islamic studies at Cambridge and director of studies in theology at Wolfson College. He is the secretary of the Muslim Academic Trust and director of the Sunna Project, based at the Centre of Middle Eastern and Islamic Studies at Cambridge University. He is a convert (or revert) to Islam, taking the name Abdal Hakim Murad; and, as one of the five Muslim scholars currently in debate with the Vatican, he is a leading Muslim academic and expositor. He is the author of *British Muslim Identity: Past, Problems, Prospects* (2003). This book is based on a lecture that was originally given in 1999 at the Royal Commonwealth Institute, at an event organised by the British Council – an 'event' indeed! The Quilliam Foundation, to which I have already referred, was founded in 2008 specifically so that 'Western Muslims should be free from the cultural baggage of the Indian subcontinent, or the political burdens of the Arab world'. Its founders are the ex-Islamists Ed Husain and Maajid Nawaz, who describe themselves as having 'travelled the paths of extremism...and [as having] resoundingly rejected Islamism while remaining committed Muslims' (Quilliam Foundation website, 18 April 2008). These young men, who have been the recipients of death threats, clearly have courage. (As well as death threats, they have, rather oddly, been on the receiving end of strictures from the liberal British press. The playwright David Edgar described them as being part of the 'culture of betrayal', which is wrecking the alliance between the British Left and Islam (*Guardian*, 19 April 2008). I have already referred to the work of Mohammad Siddique Seddon and his fellow editors of *British Muslims: Loyalty and Belonging* (2003).

They are part of a group of academics working with the Islamic Foundation and its associated institutions; in Chapter 3, I quoted from their writings on what they consider (quaintly, bizarrely, it seems to me) to be the contemporary significance to Britain of the seventh-century *hijrah* to Abyssinia. The book as a whole is, as the title shows, an attempt (yet another!) to lay Muslim title on Britishness. Lastly, in *Muslim Europe or Euro-Islam: Politics, Culture and Citizenship in the Age of Globalization* (edited in 2002 by Nezar AlSayyad and Manuel Castells), a variety of scholars, including Muslim academic Tariq Modood, make the same effort on the broader European identity. AlSayyad and Castells (who is, as far as I know, not a Muslim) are academics working in the field of architecture and planning, though AlSayyad combines this with running the Centre for Middle Eastern Studies at Berkeley, California. Tariq Modood, a leading Muslim scholar, is professor of sociology, politics and public policy at the University of Bristol. The language this last set of scholars use is rather opaque, but in essence we have the proposition that 'Muslim Europe may be the new but quintessential borderland, Euro-Islam may be [the] emerging Third space.' AlSayyad quotes, with evident agreement, Kevin Robins, a cultural historian, to the effect that in 'an opening up by Europe to non-European cultural interruption' lies the key to 'redeeming the hopes of the past'. Indeed, says Robins, without this 'a future (as opposed to a continued past) is impossible' (AlSayyad and Castells, 2002: 28). I have to admit: I have some difficulty in knowing what this means.

I will concentrate on these three or four 'schools of thought' or compilations of articles, aware that there are others, such as the British Muslims for Secular Democracy or the New Generation Network, both founded in 2006; or indeed, the 2008 Council of Ex-Muslims of Britain, whose website boldly announces: 'We Have Renounced Religion!' (This last group seems to find it possible to be moderate only by ceasing to be Muslim.) I also make use of the thoughts of Tariq Ramadan, liberal Europe's most popular Muslim (though I have yet to see a refutation of the condemnation of him made by Caroline Fourest (Fourest, 2008)), and of Yahya Birt who, like Winter, is a 'revert' to Islam after an essentially British upbringing. This assemblage of writers and academics, rather lumped together by me, all have their own particular concerns and house styles. I hope to be able to show, though, that there is, so to speak, one very large elephant in all their rooms – an elephant that makes, in their writings, only a shy and furtive appearance.

Islam, says Winter, 'is entrenching itself well' in Britain, 'becoming more British with every passing year', and 'a large Muslim presence in these islands is the most significant single event in our religious history since the Reformation' (Winter, 2003: 2). He seeks to establish the terms of 'the embedding of the religion [Islam] in the UK's historic identity' (*ibid.*: 12). This (extraordinarily enough) he sees as no great problem, and for two reasons. In the first place, Britain, he says, unlike several other European countries like Spain, Portugal, Serbia, Russia, France and even Germany, has no 'history of self-construction against an Islamic rival' – no 'reference to any Armageddon-like confrontation with Islam' (*ibid.*: 10–11). Secondly, says Winter, there is in 'traditional Sunni [Islam] a legal and theological capacity to allow conviviality and adaptation' (*ibid.*: 15), a capacity he sees demonstrated in many historical contexts, such as Poland, Lithuania, China:

> [In China] as in Poland, good Muslims consistently showed themselves to be good citizens, integrating to a high degree, but almost never succumbing to assimilation. This characteristically Muslim mode of social integration was remarkably consistent in a wide range of cultures, breaking down only when the religious Other launched policies of persecution, as with Pedro the Cruel, Ivan the Terrible or the Manchus. Such Muslim indigenizations were made possible both by the secure confidence of believers in their core identities and by the sophistication of a [Muslim/Sunni] jurisprudence which pruned and fertilized rather than supplanted.
>
> *ibid.*: 16

Note the 'only' in the second sentence of that quote. In Britain, this ataraxian Islam encountered, we are now told by Winter, a British culture with no in-built national meta-narrative that was hostile to Islam. Further, writes Winter, the British have the story of King Arthur and, while 'the [Arthurian] founding narrative of the British people is only eccentrically Christian' (*ibid.*: 19), it is the Arthurian legends, rather than the Gospels, that may provide the master narrative, the single king being transmutable into the single (i.e. non-Trinitarian) Jesus. Winter is aware that he may well be treading on several historical and theological toes: 'Few', writes Winter politely, 'believe that it would be right to adjust the Nicene resolutions to accommodate the preferences of other religionists, Muslim or otherwise' (*ibid.*: 18). He then proceeds to do just that. He insists on seeing 'a space in British christology [*sic*] which may be labelled Unitarian, and an allied soteriology which can be called Pelagian', thus making 'Islam's place far clearer and less problematic' (*ibid.*: 19). The 'only obstacle' on the Muslim side is the unfortunate vigour of the Wahhabi perspective, which has 'strong resistance to substantively embedded religion' (*ibid.*: 24). Other than that,

> From the British perspective, the arrival of Islam should be seen not as the intrusion of an essentially alien worldview, but as the augmentation of an already diverse religious landscape some of whose features have already been shaped by Islam in past centuries, and which, particularly in the tradition which I have broadly characterised as Pelagian and Platonic, is clearly hospitable to Islam's central concerns. It is for Muslims in Britain to explore and publicise this connection. To further the prosperity and integration of their important community, British Muslim leaders should consider their place not merely amid the transient landscape of race relation commissions, halal meat issues and local politics, but also amid the deep structures of national culture... For British Muslims, the past does not have to be another country.
>
> *ibid.*: 24

By 'Pelagian', I understand Winter to mean that he sees an opportunity to drop the doctrine of the Trinity and to replace it with Unitarian notions, which are more compatible with Muslim theology and which, moreover, he says, 'found more fertile ground in England than in virtually any other European country' (*ibid.*: 21). By his use of 'Platonic', Winter seems to find an opportunity to drop the doctrine of original sin, replacing it with the notion that we are born not in sin but in mere ignorance, and (more Platonism) with an inclination to strive toward the realisation and perfection of Plato's 'Forms': the search for knowledge replaces the need for salvation. Having swept all this Christian dogma out of the way, we can then, with Dr Winter, subsume Jesus Christ into King Arthur, seeing in the former an unnecessary and redundant (given the removal of original sin) practice of a full and sacrificial atonement. The Arthur/Jesus figure is to be best seen (if I follow Winter correctly) as a/the perfect ruler 'who invites transformation in his knights, not through his own self-sacrifice but through a self-discipline in grappling with the dragon of the self' (*ibid.*: 19). The Celts, Milton and Blake and early English students of Islam are adduced as contributors to the vitality of this 'archaic stratum of the British imagination' (*ibid.*). On top of this, Winter asserts that 'Britishness is certainly indefinable, and what we have traditionally taken to be its constituents are in any case subject to rapid erosion by the same globalisation that is disembedding Islam' (*ibid.*: 6). (Note how we are being eroded, rapidly, while Islam is merely 'disembedded'.)

It is actually quite hard to believe that an intelligent man like Dr Winter could find it in himself to so rubbish the history and theology of Christianity, whether here or in any other country; and to do so, moreover, in order to make more credible his thumbnail 'history' of Islam, in which Islam's enemies and only Islam's enemies are responsible for the conflicts which surround that religion. His promotion of a conjoined Jesus-cum-King Arthur as the 'archaic stratum of the British imagination' is very much closer to Muslim imaginings and archaisms about that first small band of Muslim desert warriors than it is to either Britain's religion or British history. Indeed, Yahya Birt, Winter's fellow revert, describes, in true Malory–Tolkien manner, the 'Chivalry of the Companion' and the 'Code of Chivalry [of] brotherhood, loyalty love and honour...the noble Muslim knights...the spiritual [sic] warriors who protected the boundaries of the Islamic empire' (Birt, 2001: 6–7). Birt, too, it seems, has a taste for an Arthurian (Saladinian?) 'archaic stratum', though he rather elides the fact that relations between the 'noble Muslim knights' were marked as much by assassinations and intrigues as by loyalty, love and honour. Dr Winter is a moderate man, able, in another context, to comment to fellow Muslims that they should take on board the sensible view that seeking political asylum in any Muslim country would probably be a bad idea, and that Britain is undoubtedly a better place to be (Seddon *et al.*, 2003: 20). He is British born and bred, raised, it seems, in the 'Congregational' tradition of British Dissent, the Congregationalists being once the backbone of Cromwell's New Model Army. Winter's prescription for the 'embedding' of Islam into Britain feels rather like the process whereby, centuries ago, the British 'embedded' themselves in large parts of India and Africa, by inventing artificial puppet states and puppet rulers, all of them imposed in ignorance, arrogance and indifference upon aboriginal societies whose own traditional ways of doing things were thus denied, distorted and rendered irrelevant – and made over to suit an external imposition. Hidden in T. J. Winter's very scholarly moderateness is an intellectual form of indirect rule. He might, too, spend some time on the implications of his comment about the Reformation: do we really want or need to go through all that again, just to accommodate Muhammad?

The Quilliam Foundation is a self-consciously moderate Muslim organisation, founded (in 2008) and fronted by young men from the school of hard knocks: 'we have all travelled the path of extremism'. Maajid Nawaz, co-founder of Quilliam with Ed Husain, was imprisoned and tortured in Egypt. In what follows, I quote from their initial website publicity and from my own record of the April 2008 launch, which took place in the rather grand conference centre at the British Museum, London – Quilliam is apparently funded by Kuwaiti businessmen. They say that their foundation 'rejects foreign ideologies of Islamism and Jihadism as aberrant readings of the Islamic tradition and are thus irrelevant and defunct. We uphold Islam as a pluralistic, diverse tradition that can heal the pathology of Islamist extremism.' Further, 'Western Muslims should be free from the cultural baggage of the Indian subcontinent, or the political burdens of the Arab world.' The foundation takes its name from the life and example of William Quilliam, an idiosyncratic Liverpuddlian who founded the first mosque in Britain in 1889, and 'in his memory [the foundation] is a think-tank and campaign group to help foster a British Islam, *native to these islands*, free from the bitter politics of the Arab and Muslim world' (my emphasis). (Quilliam is, perhaps, something of an odd choice: Birt sees him as being anti-British, writing 'subversive pan-Islamic tracts in favour of defensive jihad, ummatic solidarity and...of the beleaguered caliphate', and as being 'unabashed and unapologetic about his loyalties' (Birt, 2008).)

Other than the very Britishness of their figurehead, William Quilliam, the focus of the foundation seems rather more Muslim–European than British, seeking, as the founders say, to 'revive Western Islam, our Andalusian heritage of pluralism and respect, and thereby find harmony in West-Islam relations'. At the London launch, mention was made of the aim of establishing a European network of Muslims to inform civil society (Britain's Civitas think-tank is a Quilliam supporter). As models for a better way of doing things, they and one or two of their speakers referred (in no particular order) to what they considered to be the historical and exemplary societies of 12th-century Muslim Spain (*Al-Andalus*), the Ottoman Empire, medieval Baghdad and Indonesia. Professor Timothy Garton-Ash spoke of the 'extraordinary pluralism of Muslim civilisation', while Lord Paddy Ashdown (through a video link) was sure that we all hold the same fundamental values, being all the children of Abraham; 'Euro-Islam', he said, 'goes back 400 years and has no difficulty in being European.' Imam Dr Musharraf Hussain al-Azhari from Nottingham was particularly impressed with Muslim Spain, seeing it as

> a plural and harmonious society that lived there, and this is the model we want for the British Islam we want to revive here... Another model for Britain is the one in Indonesia, where modernity and Islam are fine together...this is not reforming Islam, as it doesn't need reforming, having been given us as it is by Muhammad.

Shaykh Abdel-Aziz Al-Bukhari, a Sufi master and peace campaigner from Jerusalem, felt that it was *more* difficult to create inter-faith discussions *in Europe* than it was in Israel/Palestine, as in Europe Muslims had lost their identity and it was 'hard to live in foreign and non-Muslim places without being extremist – this is difficult'. Dr Ali al-Saleh al-Najafi, from Dublin, stated that 'Muslims constructed a successful civilisation wherever they went.'

While Tim Winter (above) at least has a British focus (albeit an idiosyncratic and ahistorical one), what we were being offered by Quilliam, as a model for Britain, was only in very small measure British, being primarily and anachronistically European – and in large measure something derived from a highly partial view of *Muslim* 'history' in Europe. We can ignore, for now, the obvious incompatibility of Winter's version of British exceptionalism with Quilliam's presentation of the generally equable and peaceable nature of Muslim Europe. Muslim Spain (or *Al-Andalus*) is a consistent major presence in this ideo-historical reconstruction, incantations about its 'tolerant pluralism and vibrant intellectual life' now taken as credal – if I may be forgiven this solecism. The architecture of the Alhambra at Granada is, without doubt, stunning – indeed, 'architecture' is too small a term to embrace it: it is a wonder. Greek learning was, indeed, systematically translated into Arabic, in medieval Baghdad, and in that way 'kept alive'. Yet, while Muslim Spain was, indeed, a major repository of science and culture, the pre-eminent

Jewish writer Maimonides (Rambam) had to flee from Almohadic Spain, threatened by the Muslim 'offer' of convert or die. The great Almanzor (the 'scourge of God', 976–1031) was a great burner of books and libraries, as well as a destroyer of rival Christian states and a vigorous prosecutor of civil war. Andalusian Spain was the base for endless military expeditions against neighbouring Christian kingdoms, from which booty and slaves, male and female, were taken back to fill the households and militias of various Muslim rulers. Non-Muslims resident in Andalusia were *dhimmis*, lower class and vulnerable to endless humiliations and civic penalties, and able to escape such a life only by converting to Islam. Under the dynasties of the Umayyads, Almoravids and Almohad (i.e. from 755 to 1269), Muslim Spain conformed to Ibn Khaldun's prescriptive genealogy of states and dynasties, a cycle of creation, followed by preservation and then destruction (Ibn Khaldun, 1958: vol. 1, 344). The recipients of the unavoidable misery of stages one (by 'creation' Ibn Khaldun often meant 'conquest') and three were the *dhimmis*. Throughout these changes, Muslims stayed very firmly on top of the hierarchy, their 'pluralism' in such precarious times being as much a matter of necessity as of principle. The same is true of Abbasid Baghdad, where much of classical Greek writing was translated, under the direct and scholarly supervision of the Abbasid rulers:

> The only dominant group in Baghdad was the Abbasid family... By founding Baghdad and populating it with elements whose ideologies neutralised each other al-Mansur eliminated from the political centre the paramount Umayyad characteristic of Arab tribalism, gave himself the freedom to fashion his own political and cultural policies, and forestalled any future opposition from a socially dominant group.
>
> Gutas, 1998: 191

There were, at the Quilliam conference, two other candidates for exemplary status – the Ottoman Empire and

Indonesia. But perhaps enough has been said to indicate that it is hard to see how any of these is any more a model for Great Britain than was Winter's 'theology' for the Church of England (or, for that matter, for our Roman Catholic Church). Three of the Quilliam Foundation's favourite polities were Muslim-dominated *empires*, often at war with other Muslim empires, ruled by capricious and often unstable regimes, relying on slave and mercenary armies, and with a very clear and a very subordinate status for non-Muslims and non-Arabs. Who would be the *dhimmis* in Muslim-dominated Britain?

Even when these defects are balanced by the undoubted virtues of such societies, the fact remains that they are all irrefutably and unalterably foreign. I say this in no 'Little England' way: they are foreign – not relevant – to our national story, a story that makes us what we are, for better (often) and for worse (often, too). Parading such societies before a gathering in the United Kingdom of Great Britain and Northern Ireland (to use our national name), in the British Museum, is a tactical ploy, enabling their promoters to avoid having to face up to the very much more difficult task of, first, understanding and, second, adapting to *this* society, on *these* islands, *now*. These Muslims, moderate and well-intentioned though they are, seem unable to grasp a simple truth: that if you wish to be moderate in Great Britain, then you have first to make a serious effort to understand what Great Britain is. Preoccupation with a reinvented Muslim past is one very sure way of avoiding having to learn about the society in which you at present live. In 2005, Tariq Ramadan expostulated at a meeting of several hundred Muslims at the Regent's Park Islamic Centre: *HOW CAN YOU LIVE AMONG PEOPLE YOU DO NOT KNOW?!* (my notes). Ramadan instanced one avoidance technique: the stocking of Muslim bookshops (such as the one at the Regent's Park Centre) with books on Islam and nothing else. Another way of avoiding the task of 'being where you are' is to retreat into fantasies of long-gone, irrecoverable quasi-utopias (dystopias?) of once-upon-a-time Muslim-dominated empires: Granada upon Tyne? Another is to do what Winter did: define us into non-existence.

A further way – and one in which there is indeed much cultural resonance between moderate non-Muslims and moderate Muslims – is the 'Euro-Islam' option. This serves the same function as the earlier offerings discussed above: it avoids the crude fact of Britain; it avoids the nation state. 'Euro-Islam' is the third strand of moderation offered by Moderate Muslims; and indeed, it has the distinct advantage of being instantly recognisable and acceptable to many of my moderate, liberal friends, on whose minds Tim Winter's thoughts on Pelagianism or Ibn Khaldun's sociological analyses do not press too heavily or too frequently. As an example of the way 'Euro-Islam' is proffered both as a solvent of Muslim anxieties and as a carrier of Muslim ambitions, we now turn to the work of Nezar AlSayyad, Manuel Castells and Tariq Modood. I have, of course, already mentioned (Chapter 6) Modood's scarcely veiled desire to 'disestablish' the Church of England, which he regards as 'a minor national church, that all agree is no more than a residue and a token of a historical past' (Modood, 1992: 86). This is yet another fine example of the 'hoovering' of British history and society, and indeed an example of sheer arrogance: I would not dream of making such public comment on, say, the Islamic structure of Syria, unless my family had lived there for several generations.

'Europe' is an attractive option to such Moderate Muslims. Tariq Ramadan is an exponent of 'Islam in Europe'. Nezar AlSayyad and Manuel Castells are sure that 'Europe is once again becoming a land of Islam' (AlSayyad and Castells, 2002: 1). Note the 'once again'. On pages 9–28 of *Muslim Europe or Euro-Islam*, we learn that the EU and NATO are taking over the key functions of the (old) states; old states are breaking down into regional and sub-regional ethnicities; there is 'an increasing decoupling between the instrumentality of the state (i.e. citizenship) and the ethnic, cultural and roots of identity'. Demography is on the side of ethnic minorities, as 'Germany, like other European countries, is set to completely change its demographic structure within the next twenty years.' Europe, we learn, is set to become a 'borderland', 'an interstitial zone of displacement and deterritorialization that shapes the identity of the hybridized subject'. These border-lands are not 'fragments of the in-between [because] the most hybrid of places have moved firmly to the centre of the core'. The only problem 'with Europe today is not that it is not multiethnic but that it does not consider itself multiethnic' (*ibid.*: 1–3, 28). Not *yet*, one assumes.

This view of what Europe is – not 'European', not made of substantial nation states, not mono-Christian, not strong – is coupled with a hostile attitude to America. Most of my moderate, liberal British friends are uncomfortable with American hegemony, so perhaps there is something in common there. Muslim writers make the strongest case against America. Tariq Modood insists that 'Muslim populations suffer depredations, occupation, ethnic cleansing and massacres with little action by the civilized world or the international community. Indeed, the latter, especially American power and military hardware, is often the source of the destruction and terror' (Modood, 2001: 2). Further, 'British involvement with the United States's geopolitical projects – including the creation of Saudi-backed jihadism in Afghanistan in the 1980s as well as those following 9/11 – is certainly part of the current crisis and is putting great strain on multiculturalism' (Modood, 2005: 7). The new 'centre-left' coalition to which Modood aspires is anti-American, practically synonymous with being 'anti-war'. There is little here with which my moderate friends would disagree (though in a rather less voluble way): like many Europeans, they are rather anti-American and aware that getting involved in American 'geo-political projects' has its disadvantages.

As a geo-political construct, 'Europe' provides the opportunity to continue to deny the reality of 'nation', with its concomitant pressure to have to choose to become a 'citizen' of one country as opposed to another. The problems of loyalty are solved, therefore, by being avoided. At a 2005 Centre for Research on Nationalism, Ethnicity and Multiculturalism (CRONEM) conference, we were told that the state no longer needs a public identity, a shared Aristotelian notion of a single

Public Good, as we ground our civic life in a set of *universal* rights about which we all agree (more or less, apparently). Modern democracies (a much favoured phrase) are simply *forms of conversation*, said the speaker, and Britain is 'a multiplicity of systems of meanings', an endless set of self-negotiations. Space can be found for any 'up-front Muslim' within this conversation, with no implication at all that his ideas could be classed as bigotry. There is no need, the speaker went on, to 'make everyone British', as there is no such thing: 'being British is a relationship, not a quality or moral obligation'. Such claims on the state as we do make are made outside residual common values, which are them-selves not grounded in any form of social national contract, but are perfectly acceptable asymmetric claims, justified by reference to universal not national rights (author's own notes). Such a world is welcome to Yahya Birt, who sees in such formulations, as well as in those of Tariq Modood, proof of

> an inescapable shift to superdiversity in our globalising world...multi-logical processes by which integration may take place [allowing] for the inclusion of minorities within an expanded vision of Britishness, which (as Modood indicates) has more to do with process than with lists of core values...a process which places identities of consumption on centre-stage through the mass media and weakens civic and national identities that are primarily mediated through local and national state institutions.
>
> Birt, 2007a

'Britain' and 'Europe', conceived in this way, provide both alias and alibi. Whereas nations do exist, 'Europe' doesn't; and, even in its non-existence, it supersedes nations, which anyway shouldn't exist. Coupled with a consistent anti-Americanism, a weakened 'Europe' is able to provide a loose covering, a camouflage for a retained and reinvigor-ated ethnic or religious project, Muslim or otherwise.

Complementing this are the attitudes of liberal, moderate Europeans like my friends. They are uneasy with the nation state, seeing in it the 'nationalism' that sent their parents off to war. This nationalism they often associate with religion, 'the cause of wars', and are content to see in 'Europe' a Christianity that, if it exists at all, does so only as a spent force, split into bickering fragments, none of which wields legal muscle in any state. The last thing that Europe could ever be is a Christian theocracy. No, then, to nation state. No, then, to Christianity. Yes, then, to 'Europe', suitably eviscerated. Yes to Euro-Islam's Third Space.

As such, this 'Third Space' is very specific to post-Cold War Europe, a continent weary of a century of conflict and war, sceptical of values such as nationalism or patriotism, indifferent to religion, welcoming relativism, immured in unearned affluence and self-aggrandisement, practising a lazy form of democracy, hazily committed to international agencies such as the UN, ashamed of its own history as war-maker and imperialist, uncomfortable in the shadow of its great protector, Christian America – a Europe, in fact, in which my friends are very comfortable. 'Europe' has become something that is both wholly different from its own past and from the rip-roaring unregenerate conflict-full global present. Around it will swirl the rivalries of the 'quasi-imperial super-nations', but Old Europe can be seen, with the societies of Eastern Europe, as engaged in a unique process of stripping out the moral and political predicates of national life, replacing narrow war-competent nationalisms and monopolistic Christianity with an amiable tolerant boundary-indifferent pacifism. We can live within all great movements of our times by simply ignoring them, resting on our virtues. (I can think of few of my friends who have served in the armed forces, though many of their parents did.) Such a Euro-society can indeed be seen simply as a form of conversation – a very polite 'conversation', concerned with little but its own civility and the avoidance of offence; a conversation devoid of the commitment required through membership of a nation state. It is with and in such a conversation that people like Tim Winter,

Ed Husain and others may find themselves able to engage the moderate European. All those who are involved are sure, in a most civilised manner, that the crude, selfish and bellicose realities of nation states (never mind national Churches) are topics best ignored; and they are just as sure that nation states and Churches are nothing but crude, selfish and bellicose. A general welcome, then, for these Moderate Muslims? They do, however, have one serious problem. The moderate 'centre-liberal-left' is irreducibly 'secular', at ease only with 'privatised' religion. Its adherents did not like what happened to Salman Rushdie and they keep quiet about the 'incendiary cartoons' (what on earth *is* an incendiary cartoon?) only because they are frightened – and they *do not like being frightened*; and they do not like being frightened by Muslims, primarily because Muslims are not, by definition, at all secular. In discussions on the BBC about the stoning of women, or the meaning of this or that *hadith*, and in other learned discussions of the mysteries of Islam, my friends and I find echoes of a dangerous religiosity that we had long since come to regard as gone from our lives, as ludicrously medieval, on a par with dunking witches and making deals with the devil. As Tariq Modood, a leading Muslim academic, disingenuously puts it, the 'rise of Muslim assertiveness' has caused 'panic' and 'knee-jerk inconsistencies' among secular multiculturalists, and 'the result is a mixed up situation' (Modood, 2002: 126). Indeed, but confusion does not, Modood tells us, reign in the ranks of Muslims, as the Rushdie affair 'mobilized an impassioned activism that no previous campaign against racism had been remotely able to stir' (*ibid.*: 119). Muslims 'discovered a new community solidarity...what was striking was that even when the public rage against Muslims was at its most intense, Muslims neither sought nor were offered any special solidarity by any non-white minority' (*ibid.*). This is most reassuring, as is Modood's recognition that 'some versions of Islamism are not sufficiently respectful of fellow British citizens and the aspirations of a plural Britain' (Modood, 2005).

* * *

They sought it with thimbles, they sought it with care;
They pursued it with forks and hope;
They threatened its life with a railway-share;
They charmed it with smiles and with soap.

The elephant (in the shape of Britain) has at last made a shy appearance. In spite of their protestations about 'British Islam', the young men of Quilliam seem to prefer to find their lodestar in long-gone, semi-mythical Muslim states – anywhere but in the Britain in which they live, the Britain in which, of course, the *dhimmis* and *kafirs* are in charge. Winter is able to face up to the reality of Britain only by abstracting its history from its European context (were the struggles of our fellow-Christian states with Islam of no concern to us?), and by contriving so to vacuum out its major religious belief system as to render it unreal, non-existent. Modood simply skates around, smiling desperately at the cameras: Salman Rushdie, he tells us, has 'come to adopt a more pluralistic perspective, and one in which the Muslim presence is seen as a fact to be ignored at one's peril' (Modood, 2002: 114). Really? Where, in such a comment, is there either knowledge of, or respect for, British traditions of free speech? Where, in such remarks, is there any appreciation of the deep offence given to moderate British people by the threats to Sir Salman's life, by the abuse of the Queen or by the grotesque antics surrounding teddy bears in Sudan? We are consistently asked to 'respect' the sensitivities of Muslims. For those Moderate Muslims who wish to 'be British', the request must cut the other way, too. And part of 'respect' is to have the courtesy to know who we are. Why is it that, in the city in which I live, a recent attempt to create a 'City of Peace' elicited from the Muslim spokesman the grudging 'victimisation and prejudice can happen anywhere', whereas the Hindu spokesman's reaction was 'I came to this country 50 years ago. Newcastle has given me and my family respect, integrity and progress' (*Newcastle Evening Chronicle*, 21 May 2008)?

Tariq Ramadan was right: even these helpful, moderate Muslim scholars do not seem to know much about, nor care to know much about, the society in which they live, the people to whom they talk, the country to whose moral and material capital they lay claim. Their world, like the world of their more violent co-religionists, is Islam – an Islam that is fundamentally indifferent to us, ignorant of us, dismissive of us, careless of us. To it, all must conform; through it, all is refracted. There are no Moderate Muslims, for us, just now. If there were, why do we have to put in place government-run programmes to recruit moderate imams, similar programmes to get moderate Muslim women to deal with their not-so-moderate husbands, and yet another government programme to get young Muslims onto the moderate bandwagon? 'The government has found a way of placating Muslims in a way that will only damage us', says Yasmin Alibhai-Brown (*Guardian*, 2 May 2008). Why do all these things have to be done by the government anyway? Why do Muslims have to be placated? Why does the requisite moderateness not emerge naturally, spontaneously and graciously out of Muslim civil society? 'How', asks Yasmin Alibhai-Brown, 'is it that Sikhs and Hindus can live in a democracy but not Muslims?' (*ibid.*).

* * *

I end with a simple story. Every year, for the last 25 years or so, I spend a couple of weeks on Orkney, as 'remote' a part of the United Kingdom as you can find. Orkney is certainly remote from, and completely unknown to, Islam and Islamic history. There are no mosques on Orkney and (I would guess) very few, if any, Muslims. There is, to be sure, in the naval cemetery at Lyness, on the island of Hoy, one isolated British military gravestone marking the burial place of a 'Musalman' merchant seaman who was, I assume, a member of the crew of a British ship based at Scapa Flow in the First World War. Islam is irrelevant on Orkney, and no amount of multicultural writing and rewriting of history can make Muslims a part of the biography of those islands.

Some years ago, the terminal building at the airport at Kirkwall, capital of Orkney, was modernised. Orkney has long had an internal air network, and whereas before modernisation the terminal building was an amiable, warm, welcoming and ramshackle place, it is now a very pleasant 'state-of-the-art' modern facility. In fact, it's quite smart. In 2007, on being taken to the new airport to catch a plane back to Edinburgh, I was informed by the taxi driver that a battery of huge boulders around the approaches to the passenger lounge made it impossible to drop me off close to the main entrance. The boulders were not part of the original design for the new building. They were placed there after the attack (apparently by medically qualified Muslims) on Glasgow airport. The major and very prominent sign, therefore, of Muslim presence on Orkney is not a mosque or a bookshop, or a multicultural 'people to people' week, but a grim barbican of rocks defending the new airport at Kirkwall, calling to mind the attempt to blast apart, and murder people in, the terminal building at Glasgow airport. For the vast majority of people flying into and out of Kirkwall airport, Islam is symbolised by a semi-circle of grim boulders. Islam has come to Orkney. Well done.

REFERENCES

Abdullah, A. L. 2007. 'The secret lives of Muslim husbands', at www.islamonline.net

Ahmad, Eqbal. 2000. *Confronting Empire – interviews with David Barsamian* (London: Pluto Press).

Ahmad, F. 2001. 'Modern tradition? British Muslim women and academic achievement', *Gender and Education* 13(2).

Ahmad, M. 2007. 'Governance, structural adjustment & the state of corruption in Bangladesh', at www.ti-bangladesh.org/docs/muzaffer/muzaffer.htm

Alberuni, A. R. M. Ibn A. 2003. *Alberuni's India: An account of the religion, philosophy, literature, geography, chronology, astronomy, customs, laws and astrology of India about AD 1030*, edited by Edward Sachau, New Delhi: Indialog Publications PVT Ltd.

Ali, M. 2003. Brick Lane (QPD Paperbacks).

Al-Qaradawi, Y. 1997. The Lawful and the Prohibited in Islam [Al-Halal Wal_Haram Fil Islam] (Cairo: El Falah; London: Al-Birr Foundation).

AlSayyad, N. and Castells, M. (eds). 2002. *Muslim Europe or Euro-Islam: Politics, Culture and Citizenship in the Age of Globalization* (Lanham, MD: Lexington Books).

Anand, A. S. and Cochrane, R. 2005. 'The mental health of South Asian women in Britain: a review', *Psychology and Development Studies* 17(2): 195–214.

Ashford, S. and Timms, N. 1992. *What Europe Thinks: A Study of Western European Values* (Aldershot: Dartmouth).

Azami, I. A. 2004. *Muslim Manners: A Guide for Parents and Teachers of Muslim Children* (Leicester: UK Islamic Academy).

Barry, B. 2006. *Culture and Equality: An Egalitarian Critique of Multiculturalism* (Cambridge: Polity Press).

BBC. 2007. 'One day in Pakistan: views and news', BBC News online, 18 December, available at: http://news.bbc.co.uk/1/hi/in_depth/629/629/7136436.stm

Bhugra, D. *et al.* 1999/2000. 'Attempted suicide in West London: rates across ethnic minorities', *Psychological Medicine* 29/30.

Bin Laden, O. 2005. Messages to the World: The Statements of Osama bin Laden (New York: Verso).

Birt, Y. 2001. 'Being a Real Man in Islam: drugs, criminality and the problem of masculinity', at: www.crescentlife.com

Birt, Y. 2007a. 'Multiculturalism and the discontents of globalisation', at: www.yahyabirt.com/?p=75

Birt, Y. 2007b. 'The Islamist: A review', at: www.yahyabirt.com/?p=71

Birt, Y. 2008. 'Abdullah Quilliam: Britain's First Islamist?', at: www.yahyabirt.com/?p=136

Bostom, A. G. (ed.). 2005. *The Legacy of Jihad: Islamic Holy Wars and the Fate of Non-Muslims* (New York: Prometheus).

Brandon, J. and Hafez, S. 2008. *Crimes of the Community: Honour-Based Violence in the UK* (London: Centre for Social Cohesion).

Brierley, P. 2007. 'Muslim growth in the United Kingdom and worldwide', available at: www.lausanneworldpulse.com/trendsandstatistics/654/?pg=2

Bury, J. B. 1955. *The Idea of Progress* (New York: Dover).

Cabinet Office. 2008. *The National Security Strategy of the United Kingdom: Security in an interdependent world*, available at: www.official-documents.gov.uk/document/cm72/7291/7291.pdf

Clarence-Smith, W. G. 2006. *Islam and the Abolition of Slavery* (Oxford: Oxford University Press).

Cowherd, R. G. 1959. *The Politics of English Dissent – the Religious Aspects of Liberal and Humanitarian Reform Movements from 1815–1848* (London: Epworth Press).

Davies, J. 1995. *The Christian Warrior in the Twentieth Century* (Lampeter: Edward Mellen Press).

Davies, J. 2007. *Bonfires on the Ice: The Multicultural Harrying of Britain* (London: Social Affairs Unit).

Davies, N. 1996. *Europe: A History* (Oxford: Oxford University Press).

Delpech, T. 2007. *Savage Century: Back to Barbarism* (trans. George Holoch) (Washington DC: Carnegie Endowment for International Peace).

Dennis, N. 2005. *Cultures and Crimes: Policing in Four Nations* (London: Civitas).

Department for Innovation, Universities and Skills (DIUS). n.d. *Promoting Good Campus Relations, Fostering Shared Values and Preventing Violent Extremism in Universities and Higher Education Colleges*, at: www.dius.gov.uk/publications/extremismhe.pdf

Europol. 2007. *EU Terrorism Situation and Trend Report*, at: www.europol.europa.eu/publications/EU_Terrorism_Situation_and_Trend_Report_TE-SAT/TESAT2007.pdf

Europol. 2008. *EU Terrorism Situation and Trend Report*, at: www.europol.europa.eu/publications/EU_Terrorism_Situation_and_Trend_Report_TE-SAT/TESAT2008.pdf

FCO/Home Office/Muslim Council of Britain. 2004. *Muslims in Britain*.

Fourest, C. 2008. *Brother Tariq: the Doublespeak of Tariq Ramadan* (trans. Ioana Wieder and John Atherton) (London: Social Affairs Unit).

Gandhi, M. 2006. *Mohandas: A True Story of a Man, his People, and an Empire* (New Delhi: Penguin/Viking).

Glees, A. and Pope, C. 2005. *When Students Turn to Terror: Terrorist and Extremist Activity on British Campuses* (London: Social Affairs Unit).

Grayling, A. C. 2007. *Towards the Light: The Story of the Struggles for Liberty and Rights that Made the Modern West* (London: Bloomsbury).

Guardian. 2002. 'Muslim Britain', special report, June.

Gutas, D. 1998. Greek Thought, Arabic Culture: The Graeco-Arabic Translation Movement in Baghdad and Early Abbasid Society (2nd–4th/8th–10th centuries) (London: Routledge).

Hampson, N. 1990. *The Enlightenment* (Harmondsworth: Penguin Books).

Home Office (Bucke, T.). 1997. *Ethnicity and Contacts with the Police: Latest Findings from the British Crime Survey*, Home Office Research Findings no. 59, available at: www.homeoffice.gov.uk/rds/pdfs/r59.pdf

Home Office (Mirrlees-Black, C.). 2001a. *Confidence in the Criminal Justice System: Findings from the 2000 BCS*, Home Office Findings no. 137, available at: www.homeoffice.gov.uk/rds/pdfs/r137.pdf

Home Office (Clancy, A. *et al.*). 2001b. *Crime, Policing and Justice: The Experience of Ethnic Minorities – Findings from the 2000 BCS*, Home Office Research Study 223, available at: www.homeoffice.gov.uk/rds/pdfs/hors223.pdf

Home Office (Clancy, A. *et al.*). 2001c. *Ethnic Minorities' Experience of Crime and Policing: The 2000 British Crime Survey*, available at: www.homeoffice.gov.uk/rds/pdfs/r146.pdf

Home Office (Flood-Page, C. and Taylor, J.). 2003a. *Crime in England and Wales 2001/2002: Supplementary Volume*, available at: www.homeoffice.gov.uk/rds/pdfs2/hosb103.pdf

Home Office (Aust, R. and Smith, N.). 2003b. Ethnicity and Drug Use: Key Findings from the 2001/2002 British Crime Survey, available at: www.homeoffice.gov.uk/rds/pdfs2/r209.pdf

Home Office (Nicolas, S. and Walker, A.). 2004. *Crime, Disorder and the Criminal Justice System: Supplementary Volume 2*, available at www.homeoffice.gov.uk/rds/pdfs2/hosb0204.pdf

Home Office (Allen, J. *et al.*). 2005. *Policing and the Criminal Justice System – Public Confidence* and *Perceptions: Findings from the 2003/04 British Crime Survey*, available at: www.homeoffice.gov.uk/rds/pdfs05/rdsolr3105.pdf

Home Office (Allen, J. *et al.*). 2006a. *Policing and the Criminal Justice System – Public Confidence and Perceptions: Findings from the 2004/05 British Crime Survey*, available at www.homeoffice.gov.uk/rds/pdfs06/rdsolr0706.pdf

Home Office (Jansson, K.). 2006b. *Black and Minority Ethnic Groups' Experiences and Perceptions of Crime, Racially Motivated Crime and the Police: Findings from the 2004/05 British Crime Survey*, available at: www.homeoffice.gov.uk/rds/pdfs06/rdsolr2506.pdf

Home Office (Jansson, K. *et al.*). 2007. *Attitudes, Perceptions and Risks of Crime: Supplementary Volume 1 to Crime in England and Wales 2006/07*, available at: www.homeoffice.gov.uk/rds/pdfs07/hosb1907.pdf

Home Office (Kershaw, C. *et al.*). 2008. *Crime in England and Wales 2007/08: Findings from the British Crime Survey and Police Recorded Crime*, available at: www.homeoffice.gov.uk/rds/pdfs08/hosb0708.pdf

Hoodbhoy, P. A. 2007. 'Science and the Islamic world', *Physics Today*, August: 49–55 (also available at: www.richarddawkins.net).

Howe, I. 1976. *World of Our Fathers: The Journey of the East European Jews to America and the Life They Found and Made* (London: Phoenix Press).

Husain, E. 2007. *The Islamist* (Harmondsworth: Penguin Books).

Hussain, Imtiaz Ahmed. 2003. 'Migration and settlement: a historical perspective of loyalty and belonging', in Mohammad Siddique Seddon *et al.*, *British Muslims: Loyalty and Belonging* (Leicester: Islamic Foundation; London: Citizen Organising Foundation).

Ibn Khaldun. 1958. *The Muqaddimah – An Introduction to History* (first published c. AD 1396) (trans. Frank Rosenthal) Bollingen Series XLIII (New York: Pantheon Books).

iCoCo (Institute of Community Cohesion). 2008. *Understanding and Appreciating Muslim Diversity: Towards Better Engagement and Participation*, available at: www.coventry.ac.uk/researchnet/external/content/1/c4/25/58/v1208436787/user/Muslim%20Diversity%2052pp%20-%20final%20for%20web.pdf

International Crisis Group (ICG). 2006. *Bangladesh Today*, Asia Report no. 121, available at: www.crisisgroup.org/home/index.cfm?id=4462&l=1

International Crisis Group. 2008. *Restoring Democracy in Bangladesh*, Asia Report no. 151, available at: www.crisisgroup.org/home/index.cfm?id=5408&l=1

Israeli, R. 2003. *Islamikaze: Manifestations of Islamic Martyrology* (London and New York: Frank Cass).

Jefferson, T. and Walker, M. A. 1993. 'Attitudes to the police of ethnic minorities in a provincial city', *British Journal of Criminology* 33(2): 251–66.

Larkin, P. 1988. *Collected Poems* (ed. Anthony Thwaite) (London: Faber).

Lewis, B. (ed.). 1976. *The World of Islam: Faith, People, Culture* (London: Thames and Hudson).

Lewis, P. 1994. *Islamic Britain – Religion, Politics and Identity among British Muslims* (London: I. B. Tauris).

Lucan. 1992. *Civil War* (Oxford: Oxford University Press).

Maalouf, A. 1984. *The Crusades Through Arab Eyes* (trans. Jon Rothschild) (London: Al Saqi Books).

MacEoin, D. 2007. The hijacking of British Islam: how extremist literature is subverting mosques in the UK, available at: www.policyexchange.org.uk/images/libimages/307.pdf

Macey, M. 1999. 'Class, gender and religious influences on changing patterns of Pakistani Muslim male violence in Bradford', *Ethnic and Racial Studies* 22(5).

Macey, M. 2002. 'Interpreting Islam: young Muslim men's involvement in criminal activity in Bradford' in B. Spalek, *Islam, Crime and Criminal Justice* (Cullompton: Willan Publishing).

MacIntyre, A. 1967. *Secularization and Moral Change* (Oxford: Oxford University Press).

Marx, K. and Engels, F. 1848. *The Communist Manifesto*, available at: www.marxists.org/archive/marx/works/1848/communist-manifesto/

Mernissi, Fatima. 1995. *The Harem Within: Tales of a Moroccan Girlhood* (London: Bantam Books).

Mirza, M. *et al.* 2007. *Living Apart Together, British Muslims and the Paradox of Multiculturalism*, available at: www.policyexchange.org.uk/images/libimages/246.pdf

Modood, T. 1992. *Not Easy Being British: Colour, Culture and Citizenship* (London: Runnymede Trust and Trentham Books).

Modood, T. 2001. 'Muslims in the West: A Positive Asset', available at www.ssrc.org/sept11/essays/modood.htm

Modood, T. 2002. 'The place of Muslims in British secular multiculturalism', in N. Alsayyad and M. Castells (eds), *Muslim Europe or Euro-Islam: Politics, Culture and Citizenship in the Age of Globalization* (Lanham MD: Lexington Books).

Modood, T. 2005. Remaking multiculturalism after 7/7, available at: www.opendemocracy.net/conflict-terrorism/multiculturalism_2879.jsp

Modood, T. and Berthoud, R. (eds). 1997. *Ethnic Minorities in Britain: Diversity and Disadvantage. The Fourth National Survey of Ethnic Minorities* (London: Policy Studies Institute).

Muslim Directory. 2007/08. Available at: www.muslimdirectory.co.uk

Pamuk, O. 2004. *Snow* (London: Faber and Faber).

Pew Global Attitudes Project. 2006a. 'The great divide: how westerners and Muslims view each other', available at: http://pewglobal.org/reports/display.php?ReportID=253

Pew Global Attitudes Project. 2006b. 'Muslims in Europe: economic worries top concerns about religious and cultural identity', available at: http://pewglobal.org/reports/display.php?ReportID=254

Pipes, D. 1999. '[Al-Hudaybiya and] lessons from the Prophet Muhammad's diplomacy', *Middle East Quarterly*, September.

Prunier, G. 2007. 'Khartoum's calculated fever', available at: www.opendemocracy.net/article/democracy_power/khartoum_calculated_fever

Pryor, F. L. 2007. 'Are Muslim countries less democratic?', *Middle East Quarterly* XIV(4).

Putnam, R. D. 2007. 'E pluribus unum: diversity and community in the 21st century', *Journal of the Nordic Political Science Association* 30(2): 137–74.

Quick, Abdullah Hakim. n.d. (DVD) *The Devil's Deception in the New World Order* and *Islam, Past, Present and Future* (covering his lecture to the Daawah Association of Western Australia), obtainable from www.simplyislam.com

Ramadan, T. 2004. *Islam, the West and the Challenges of Modernity* (Leicester: Islamic Foundation).

Samad, M. and Eade, J. 2002. *Community Perceptions of Forced Marriage*, available at: www.fco.gov.uk/resources/en/pdf/pdf1/fco_forcedmarriagereport121102

Seddon, M., Hussain, D. and Malik, N. 2003. *British Muslims: Loyalty and Belonging* (Leicester: Islamic Foundation; London: Citizen Organising Foundation).

Serck, L. 2004. 'Emel: a Muslim lifestyle magazine', BBC online, at: www.bbc.co.uk/berkshire/faith/06/emel_magazine.shtml

Shari'ati, Ali. 1986. What Is to Be Done: The Enlightened Thinkers and an Islamic Renaissance (Houston TX: Institute for Research and Islamic Studies).

Sharma, H. D. (ed.). 1998. *100 Best Pre-Independence Speeches 1870–1947* (New Delhi: Harper Collins).

Siddiqui, K. 1983. *Issues in the Islamic Movement, 1981–82 (1401–1402)* (London: Open Press).

Sieny, M. E. 2000. *Heroes of Islam* (Riyadh: Darussalam Publishing House).

Spalek, B. 2002. *Islam, Crime and Criminal Justice* (Cullompton: Willan Publishing).

Stern, J. P. 1992. *The Heart of Europe* (Oxford: Blackwell).

Thomas, W. I. and Znaniecki, F. (eds). 1996. *The Polish Peasant in Europe and America* (Urbana: University of Illinois Press).

Thomson, A. and Ata'ur-Rahim, M. 1996. *Islam in Andalus* (London: Ta-Ha Publishers).

Transparency International. 2006. Pakistan – National Corruption Perception Survey, available at: www.transparency.org.pk/documents/National%20Corruption%20Perception%20Survey%202006.pdf

Trevane, J. 2004. *Fatwa: Living with a Death Threat* (London: Hodder and Stoughton).

UN Development Programme (UNDP). 2007. *Human Development Report 2007/2008*, available at: http://hdr.undp.org/en/media/HDR_20072008_EN_Complete.pdf

US Department of State (Bureau of Democracy, Human Rights and Labor). 2007. Country Report on Human Rights Practices, Bangladesh, released 11 March 2008, available at: www.state.gov/g/drl/rls/hrrpt/2007/100612.htm

Wilkinson, A. 1978. *The Church of England and the First World War* (London: SPCK).

Winter, T. J. 2003. *British Muslim Identity: Past, Problems, Prospects* (Cambridge: Muslim Academic Trust).

WEBSITES

Anti-Slavery International: www.antislavery.org/
Barnabas Fund: www.barnabasfund.org/
Capital punishment worldwide information: http://encarta.msn.com/
    media_461543496/capital_punishment_worldwide.html
Central Intelligence Agency, *World Factbook*: https://www.cia.gov/library/
    publications/the-world-factbook/
Centre for Research on Nationalism, Ethnicity and Multiculturalism
    (CRONEM), University of Surrey and the University of Roehampton:
    www.surrey.ac.uk/Arts/CRONEM/
Daily Telegraph: www.telegraph.co.uk/
Daniel Pipes website: www.danielpipes.org/
Dhimmi Watch: http://jihadwatch.org/dhimmiwatch/archives/002775.php
Institute of Objective Studies *Minaret* online Islamic magazine:
    www.iosminaret.org/
International Crisis Group: www.crisisgroup.org/home/index.cfm
Islam for Today: www.islamfortoday.com/
Islam Online: www.islamonline.net/english/index.shtml
Islamist Watch website: www.islamist-watch.org/
Lausanne World Pulse: www.lausanneworldpulse.com/
Ministry of Justice: www.justice.gov.uk/
Musings on the Britannic Crescent (Yahya Birt): www.yahyabirt.com/
Muslim Council of Britain (MCB): www.mcb.org.uk/
Muslim Directory: www.muslimdirectory.co.uk
Muslim Safety Forum (MSF): www.muslimsafetyforum.org/
Muslim Weekly: www.themuslimweekly.com
Observer Human Rights Index: www.guardian.co.uk/rightsindex
Open Democracy: www.opendemocracy.net/
Pew Global Attitudes Project: http://pewglobal.org/
Pink Islam: www.pinkislam.com
Populus polls: www.populuslimited.com/
Press Freedom Index: www.rsf.org/rubrique.php3?id_rubrique=20
Qatar Foundation *Awraq* newsletter archive: www.qf.org.qa/output/
    Page1870.asp
Quilliam Foundation: www.quilliamfoundation.org/
Royal United Services Institute for Defence and Security Services (RUSI):
    www.rusi.org

Shelina's blog – Islam Online: www.islamonline.net/servlet/
Satellite?c=Article_C&cid=1199279969826&pagename=Zone-English-
Family%2FFYELayout

Silchar community website: www.silchar.com

Sunna Project: www.ihsanetwork.org

Sylheti Matrimony: www.sylhetimatrimony.com/

Transparency International: www.transparency.org/

Umm Layth, muslimah blog: http://ummlayth.muslimpad.com/
2007/06/18/dont-be-ashamed-of-being-a-muslimah/

UN Development Programme – Human Development Index: http://
hdr.undp.org/en/statistics/indices/hdi/

UN Food and Agriculture Organization information on food insecurity in
the world: www.fao.org/SOF/sofi/

UN Food and Agriculture Organization information on low-income food-
deficit countries (LIFDC): www.fao.org/countryprofiles/lifdc.asp

UN Office of the High Representative for the Least Developed Countries:
www.un.org/ohrlls/

US Department of State country reports on human rights practices (2007):
www.state.gov/g/drl/rls/hrrpt/2007/

World Economic Forum, Global Competitive Index 2007/08:
www.gcr.weforum.org/